M000196849

Life Interrupted

Encountering the Unexpected

LISA Q. HERRIN

Life Interrupted

Encountering the Unexpected

LIVING INK
BOOKS
Writing Worth Reading

ISBN 0-89957-174-3

First printing—September 2005

Cover designed by ImageWright, Inc., Chattanooga, Tennessee. Interior design and typesetting by Reider Publishing Services, West Hollywood, California. Edited and Proofread by Melanie Rigney, Dan Penwell, Donna Clark Goodrich, and Rick Steele

---

Library of Congress Cataloging-in-Publication Data

Herrin, Lisa Q., 1961-
  Life interrupted : encountering the unexpected / Lisa Q. Herrin.
      p. cm.
  Summary: "Uses the personal experiences of the author and others to encourage the reader to have hope when the unexpected events of life, such as unfair demands on our time, death, and suffering, come in their lives"-- Provided by publisher.
   ISBN-13: 978-0-89957-174-4 (pbk. : alk. paper)
   ISBN-10: 0-89957-174-3 (pbk. : alk. paper)
   1. Christian life. 2. Life change events. I. Title.
BV4501.3.H47 2005
248.8'6--dc22
                                        2005018296

Printed in the United States of America

11 10 09 08 07 06 05 –B– 8 7 6 5 4 3 2 1

To my husband, Robert,
in whose honesty, faithfulness, and love I find rest

Contents

Acknowledgments

MANY THANKS to all my dear loved ones for making this book possible, and to God who offered me this wonderful privilege.

An extra special thank you to—

My family:

Robert—my dear heart and the reason I'm writing
Joe—my dearest only son
Latese and Philip—priceless friendship
Torrey and Polly—for allowing me into the family
Noah, Karson, and Schaunie—I love you the most
Mom and Dad—for wonderful memories

Teresa and Stan—a listening ear
Kenneth—your many prayers
Darrell and Donna—Giving hope
Jennifer, Michael Lee, Jason, and Megan—so much fun
Chester and Mattie—for a precious son, Steve
Don and Jackie—for loving me
Willis and Peachy—for liking my first discourse

My prayer partners:
Bunny Shelton, Lori Goff, and Mary Kolodziej

My special friends and fellow writers:
Brenda Douglas, Lorrie Welborn, Cheryl Johnston, Waneda Brownlow, Peggy Morris, and Jeff Friend

The Plant City Church of God:
For allowing me to fulfill my purpose without complaint—even when I missed some of your baby and wedding showers

My editor and friend:
Dan Penwell—for first believing in this book

CHANGED PLANS
Overshadowing
Interruptions

Give me a pure heart—
that I may see Thee,
A humble heart—
that I may hear Thee,
A heart of love—
that I may serve Thee,
A heart of faith—
that I may abide in Thee.

Thou takest the pen—
and the lines dance.
Thou takest the flute—
and the notes shimmer.
Thou takest the brush—
and the colors sing.

So all things have meaning and beauty in that space
Beyond time where Thou art.
How, then, can I hold back anything from Thee.[1]

—DAG HAMMARSKJÖLD

Chapter
ONE

We Now Interrupt This Life
Why Interruptions

THE GARAGE felt like a hundred degrees. What a stupid idea to hang curtains over the garage door windows. My husband, Steve, didn't understand either. I remembered our discussion from the previous evening.

"Why do you need frilly curtains in my workshop?"

For the third time I explained, "It's not for the inside, but the outside. Look at the other windows in front of the house. Lovely ruffled curtains frame every window with a heart attached to the center windowpane. They're beautiful. Everybody's doing it."

He looked outside the window. Well, maybe not everybody in our neighborhood.

While Steve worked, I took the opportunity to hang my curtains. I knew he'd adore them once he saw how nicely they looked when he entered the drive. But it was so hot.

I had purchased four spring rods to help accomplish the task. I hammered and turned the screws as perspiration ran down my back.

"Ouch! You stupid rod!" The wood was soft in some areas. When I attached the flexible rod to one end, the other end broke loose and smacked my face.

"Mom-m-m-m! Hey Mom-m-m-m! Derek won't let me ride my bike."

"Joe, why don't you march out there and tell him it's your bike and you'll share, but now it's your turn? Now go along I'm busy."

Whack! Red-faced, I rubbed my wounded cheek as perspiration stung my eyes. *Who would make such a ridiculous garage door? I should return this stupid contraption to the company. It can't even hold a screw.*

"Mom, Derek still won't let me ride my bike!"

"Joe, knock Derek off of the bike and take it back!"

He charged out the door. *Oh no, what have I done? Derek is twice his size. He'll kill Joe.* I hurried to preempt him. Just as I opened the door, I saw my little five-year-old son standing in the middle of the front yard with his hands on his hips screaming at Derek and Derek's parents.

"My mama told me to knock you off of my-y-y-y-y bike."

Mom was busted. With my head slightly lowered, I smiled at everyone and helped Joe retrieve his bike. We entered the house, where I apologized for uttering such foolish words.

I managed to hang the curtains before Steve arrived home, and he liked them, as least I think he did.

Interruptions Frustrate

Interruptions annoy us. Could anything be more important than the project we're working on? Some people don't think so. They never outgrow their childhood urge to interrupt. They call, but never ask if we're eating dinner; they interrupt our conversations; and they enter our office at the most inconvenient times. Our food is cold before we have a chance to speak, our point is lost, and we forget what we're doing when we're interrupted.

I once attended a tent sale. I arrived as the sale began, but the crowd was immense. After I finished shopping, I got in line to pay for my merchandise. At that point the line wrapped halfway around the tent from the checkout. A lady approached a customer behind me with a clever excuse to break line, which met with a reprimand.

"I must be somewhere and I'll be late for my appointment. Would you please allow me to step in front of you?"

"Lady, we all have appointments. You should have thought about that before you wasted your time shopping. The line is back there." She pointed her finger to the back of the line. "And I suggest you start moving."

Although I didn't see myself delivering such a lecture, I secretly enjoyed hers. It was as if she were repaying every woman who had ever broken line in front of me.

Interrupted. What's so annoying about someone wheeling her cart in front of me while I'm waiting in line at the grocery store? I feel ignored. It's as if I were two feet tall in a six-foot world—like a child again. I touch my skin to see if I'm invisible. When I'm interrupted in this manner, it evokes feelings of worthlessness. The other party devalues my need to hurry home, prepare dinner, clean the dishes, wash laundry, relax with family, have devotions, and crash. She thinks her meatloaf tastes better, her children more valuable, her house prettier. What do I do?

I refuse to be passive by pretending such behavior is acceptable. Maybe if the attempted line breaker would turn around, I could cast an evil eye that says: *You inconsiderate female goat-head.* But she'll never look back. So, I consider calling my husband on the cell phone and say, "I would be home BUT . . . this woman stepped in line in front of me. I mean *right in front of me.*" When I feel better, I forgive her. She's just a sinner. A Christian lady wouldn't do such an unthinkable thing—would she?

Like Internet pop-up ads, interruptions invade our perimeters in many colors. Whether it's someone sipping coffee at a green light, a train changing tracks, or the eleventh telephone solicitor of the day calling, we own a life and somebody is preventing us from enjoying it. Our daily planners stay compacted with parent-teacher conferences, business appointments, community meetings, church activities, car care, hair care, dental care, nail care, baby showers, wedding showers, new home showers, birthday parties, graduation parties, and anniversary parties. Then we consider the ordinary day—bills to pay, clothes to fold, grass to cut, dishes to wash, beds to make, meals to cook, and floors to sweep. Do we have time for interruptions? I didn't think so the afternoon Jessica called.

The call came before caller ID became a reality. What if it was Mom, or Joe from school, or our next-door neighbor? I must answer. At the sound of Jessica's voice, my heart sank.

She had many problems, among those being the deployment of her military husband. This call announced yet another crisis. A fire had destroyed her home. At the moment I didn't feel emotionally able to care for her. Yet, I felt responsible to help. So, temporarily, I took Jessica into my home until she arranged other living accommodations.

We were greatly inconvenienced by this arrangement. Jessica scrambled our plans. Breakfast, lunch, and dinner seemed uncertain. And what about the bathroom?

Do we ever plan to be interrupted? Do we anticipate a call at 2:00 a.m. to inform us of a dear friend's death in a car accident? Do we organize a crisis to begin at precisely the same time as the evening news? Do we open the front door in the morning expecting someone to burst into our home to interrupt our breakfast? Definitely not! We never invite interruptions into our lives.

Interruptions are a nuisance. They annoy us because they occur outside the routine of ordinary events. Interruptions do not navigate well into our busy schedules. They are like a prick with a needle, the sting of a bee, a nagging toothache, a sledgehammer to our big toe. We hate interruptions because they can't be controlled.

Regardless of our clever arrangements, we cannot stop an airplane from diving into an office complex. We cannot revive the dead. We cannot retrieve the little girl's daddy. We cannot force evil men to love. We cannot right every wrong. We cannot rewind the course of events. Interruptions shock us, humble us, devastate us, and confuse us. An interruption can change our life.

Interruptions Evoke Reevaluation

I sat watching football with my husband Steve. His team was on the one-yard line, first and goal. On the second play, the opposing team intercepted the ball. Steve threw up his hands in disgust. When I laughed, Steve sent a murderous look in my direction.

What struck me as humorous? Life. We have it all figured out. We're certain of a touchdown. We taste sweet victory and then we're suddenly swamped with defeat. But it isn't always funny.

If it were possible to write out our life, we'd plan it perfectly without interruptions. We'd decide when to meet Mr. Right. We'd plan our wedding for a sunny spring day. We'd honeymoon in Bermuda and it wouldn't rain. We'd time the arrival of our first child at the most convenient time—when we had good-paying jobs, a large home with a fenced-in yard, and a minivan parked in the garage. But for all our well-thought-out plans, it doesn't happen as we expect. We meet the man of our dreams after many years of prayer and our first child arrives when our husband's company goes under.

We plan to succeed and we fail. We plan to prosper and we go bankrupt. We plan to marry and we remain single. We plan to have children and we're childless. We plan to build and our plans fall into an ashen heap. We wonder why.

Alongside plans, we develop routines. We develop a list of favorite entrees at our favorite restaurants and we make regular visits. But then it's removed from the menu and we must decide upon another selection. We resist these choices. We'd rather have the linguini with Alfredo sauce, chicken, and sundried tomatoes.

Interruptions are inevitable and our mental well-being

plays a role in how well we handle them. Women have been known to become pregnant at forty-five with grandchildren living next door. But such a woman can't make the pregnancy disappear, so she adjusts. She decides on a name. She strips away the guest room wallpaper and begins a search for baby furnishings and paint. She purchases a new car that the baby seat will fit into and replaces her mid-life Corvette. Then she rolls along. She simply must.

Interruptions Define Us

Interruptions define who we are and what we believe. They meet us in unexpected places and they reveal unexpected responses. Will I come through for a friend who is hurting? How much of my world evolves around me and how much of it includes others?

As babies, we scream when we're in pain, wet, hungry, or lonely, and we depend on others to meet these needs. As we grow older, we learn to extend our bottle, pacifier, and cherished toy to others. We enter a new world of understanding when we recognize others' needs. The number of interruptions dramatically increases when we allow people into our intimate space—a situation Jesus knew much about.

Jesus took possession of his life and laid it down for us. He was interrupted in every conceivable way. He couldn't share one decent conversation, deliver a simple sermon, or travel to a specific location without an interruption. The amazing part about Jesus' interruptions is that he handled them with ease, as if they were not interruptions. Joanna Weaver explains Jesus' motivation of compassion:

Jesus didn't respond to the people out of duty; he ministered to them because he felt their distress. So deep, so profound was his compassion, his *splagchnizomai,* Jesus literally felt it in his gut. He laid aside his hurt so he could pick up their pain. He laid aside his wishes so he could become their one Desire. He laid aside his agenda so he could meet all of their needs.[2]

However, the disciples, like us, held a more earthly perspective on interruptions. They considered them distractions. Whether Jesus was interrupted by a Syrophenician woman, a blind Bartimaeus, a woman holding costly perfume, or rambunctious children, the disciples felt Jesus' current involvement was an intrusion. The sermon was more important, travel was more important, adults were more important, solitude was more important, conversations were more important, meals were more important.

But Jesus knew that people were more important.

Interruptions As Opportunities

Jesus saw the man being lowered through the ceiling of a house as an opportunity to illustrate faith. He saw the interruption of the storm as an inroad to prove peace is ours in the turmoil of life. He viewed the interruption of the Pharisees as a means to teach the truth. Although everyone viewed the cross as the greatest interruption of mankind, Jesus embraced it. Jesus knew this was no interruption.

All this made me wonder how many incidents in my life that I had interpreted as interruptions were in fact opportunities? Were my encounters with strife opportunities for growth? Maybe the phone call wasn't an interruption, but a signal that I needed to sit and visit with a friend. It felt good when I did.

Our lives are rapidly rolling. We don't take kindly to interruptions. We are in cahoots with the disciples. Can you imagine yourself in a jet airplane shouting at Bartimaeus, "Hey man! Don't you see we have somewhere to go? We'll catch you later. We have no time to waste."

Would you be angry with the men cutting a hole in your roof and demand that it be repaired immediately? What about the time spent repairing it? Would you be worried sick that it wouldn't be repaired before rain came?

I enjoy bargain shopping—especially those sales where I take an "additional 25 percent off" the already marked down price. I can't imagine the outrage I'd feel regarding a woman pouring an entire, full-priced bottle of expensive perfume over Jesus when just a dab would have worked. Surely, Jesus must have felt the same. He didn't tolerate waste either.

Oh, how I'd hate his rebuke—maybe not the words, but the look of disappointment when I failed to comprehend that *people* were more important than things.

Some of us spend our lives glaring at the irritating interruption. We struggle to stomp it out beneath our feet. We don't want to change, but we want our situation to change. We don't want to move, but we want others to move. We don't want to share, forgive, or repent, yet we want our fill of blessing. We struggle to receive the message of interruptions, although it screams at us daily. We refuse to understand that our response to the interruption determines the outcome. Jerry Cook and Stanley Baldwin say:

Non-pressured living has become almost a god in our world. If you design a life free of pressures, you probably also will have a life of mediocrity. Count on it: without pressure there is little change, and without change there can be no growth.[3]

We tend to avoid interruptions because we disdain powerless situations. Our well-ordered world allows no intruders who refuse to follow our rules. We're convinced we've purchased happiness.

Interruptions and the God Piece

Maybe we've laid our lives on a table in segmented pieces and contemplated how they should fit. We don't know what to do with the God piece, so we push it to the side. We understand the Sunday morning ritual, the occasional weeknight service, the quick prayers, and the brief devotionals, but obedience confuses us. We don't understand God's expectations. We settle for comfort.

We build massive rooms for comfortable places—the Sunday nap, the big screen TV, the afternoon sunbath, the cake decorating class, the jewelry party, the women's luncheon. With the temporary removal of one cushion, we convince ourselves unhappiness will soon follow. Yet, in the hidden crevices of our heart a longing for more continues. The God piece fits somewhere.

Our children interrupt us for a piece of the action, a piece of our conversation, a piece of our cake, a piece of our jewelry, a piece of our pillow, a piece of our time.

Our husband interrupts us. To meet his desire for admiration, we clap; for his need of support, we offer a hand; for his want of gratitude, we say kind words. When we've met our husband's needs, fed our children, and attempted to satisfy ourselves, we look to the doorway. God is still there. But it's time for bed. We go to sleep knowing a change must occur.

If you're close to forty, in your forties, or pushing fifty, you've probably experienced enough of the routine ruts, small hints of happiness, and mundane mood swings. Do you concern yourself with thoughts of heaven—going there with nothing to offer Jesus? I have. I've been creeping past forty for several years now. As each day passes, my restlessness grows. If all goes well, people my age will have another thirty years. Are these years enough to fulfill our dreams? We can't take a chance, too much is at stake. We must move quickly. Are you ready to bust loose? I definitely am.

Don't suffocate me in a closet, but let me skydive from Mount Everest. Let my cheeks feel the icy sting of my descent. I want to plunge into the depths of the Atlantic and know I have touched life when I caress the coral on the surface of the ocean floor. Don't force me to life in passivity while the circus leaves town. Allow me to ride the elephant, tame the lion, laugh with the clown, and then cry when it's all ended. I want to know I have lived before I die.

Take me to the valley of dead bones and allow me to witness my resurrection. Let me behold God on a throne surrounded by seraphim. Allow me to weave my way through the crowd to grasp his precious robe. Place me in the Garden of Gethsemane to hear again my beloved Savior's final prayer. Clothe me in priestly attire. Escort me to the holy place and deliver me before the ark of his presence. Please let me stay here awhile.

Could our greatest interruption be God—the piece we can't figure out? The piece we've placed to the side. The piece that makes all the other pieces fit perfectly. The piece that sets us free—the most important piece.

Why don't you pick it up? Don't be afraid. Inspect it. Close your hand around it. Hold it near your heart. See how nicely it fits. Rest just a moment. Lean your head against his chest and hear his heartbeat. Oh, how Jesus loves you.

God's Plan

Look outside your window. God's plan for your life is waiting there. It's coming forward to shake your hand. Let it happen. You'll never be fulfilled until it happens. Don't live your entire life, missing the mark. His plans seem a little scary, but know that he has confidence in you. If he didn't, he wouldn't ask.

What is he telling you to do? Take neighborhood children to church? Teach a Sunday school class? Begin a clothing ministry for the poor? Lead an office Bible study? Arise an hour early to pray? Send money to a missionary? Mow your enemy's grass, care for her baby, buy her groceries? Volunteer at the hospital? Write a book, an article, a letter? He isn't asking anyone else. Just you.

Earlier, I mentioned making curtains for my home. Not only did I make curtains for my home, but also for my friends, my mother, my mother-in-law, my sister, and my sisters-in-law. I felt God called me to the curtain-making ministry. I felt sure he'd bring countless people my way to minister to through this amazing endeavor. Daily, I had church as I revved up the volume on my tape player to drown out the steady hum of the

Kenmore sewing machine. I liked making curtains. But then one day everything changed.

As a housewarming gift, I offered to make my dear friend floor-length drapes for her entire house. We measured her windows and visited the fabric store to purchase her cream-colored material and sewing notions. I designed a pattern, placed the fabric against it, and cut them. With the equipment organized, away I sped along on another mission.

Toward the middle of the week, an amazing thing brought my curtain-making ministry to a grinding halt. Somewhere between the stitches, God interrupted me with an amazing revelation. *Lisa, I didn't call you to the curtain-making ministry. I'm calling you to study to teach my Word.*

A horrible dread closeted me as I looked around the small room at the numerous piles of unsewn fabric. *God isn't pleased with this,* I thought. The project appeared endless. I didn't want to be outside of God's will, as was the case for many days. Eventually the curtains were completed and my friend rejoiced over them. But I wasn't the same anymore.

While my idea for ministry felt okay, God's idea felt *great.* While I enjoyed sewing, I loved studying. During the course of an ordinary day, God spoke. And I said, *Speak again.* And he did, many times when I least expected it—through a book, via a friend, in his Word, in music, or through a sermon—as I cleaned and listened to a tape. *Oh God, please interrupt me. Your interruptions are the very best kind.* But then is God ever an interruption. Isn't he always first?

Maybe the whole issue of annoyance over interruptions is wrapped up in our perceived time restraints. Nancy Leigh

DeMoss refers to our idea concerning lack of time to complete tasks as areas we must reevaluate.

> There is virtually never time in a twenty-four-hour day for me to do everything that is on everyone else's "to do" list for me. There is seldom time to do everything that is on my own "to do" list. I cannot meet with every person who wants an appointment, call every person who wants to talk, counsel with every person who has a need, tackle every project that people think I would be good at, read all the books I'd like to read, spend the kind of time I'd like to spend with my friends, and keep every room in my house presentable for guests who drop in. It's just not physically possible.
>
> What a relief to realize I don't have to do all those things! The truth is that all I have to do is the work God assigns to me. What a freedom it has been for me to accept that there is time for me to do everything that is on God's "to do" list for my day, for my week, and for my life.[4]

As a girl, I always wanted my friends to meet my dad. I thought he was made of elastic. He still possesses an amazing resiliency. My younger brother, Ken, says Dad is the happiest man he has ever met. He enjoys a good laugh, even at his own expense. He never outgrew his need to be a child. If I'm home, he tickles my feet to get me on my way or splashes a little faucet water in my face to ensure he has my attention. Even at seventy-seven, he thinks he can wrestle me to the ground. Interruptions don't mean much to him. He just snaps his fingers, does a little jig, and leaps right over them. You should see him. He really does.

He'd say, "Don't allow interruptions to defeat you." Like frogs floating in formaldehyde, learn to take them out of the jar and dissect them. What's inside is pretty amazing.

Don't circle the city, but learn to manage the traffic. Maybe the interruption is a God-thing clothed in traffic jams offering another few moments of quiet to worship him. Maybe the interruption is a rainy day bringing rest. Maybe it's the ring of your doorbell presenting a dozen roses. Maybe it's a toddler's tumble capturing a picture of lasting memories. Then maybe it's an angel stopping the bullet intended for you—presenting you with another chance.

I Can Do Something About This

I can do everything through him who gives me strength
(Philippians 4:13).

Pray
Dearest Lord,
At times my life is stressful. I don't want to live this way because
stress clouds my perspectives and steals my joy and prevents me
from fulfilling my purpose. With your help, I will complete the
following steps because I desire to change. I trust you to speak
concerning any area of my life that needs correction.

Commit
I will not say, "I can't," because God says, "I can."

Question
Is my life stressful? On a sheet of paper
list the areas most stressful to you.

Analyze
Look at each stress individually. Take the first one.
Explain why this is stressful. Do the same with the others.

Plan
Put aside money for a two-hour vacation.

Go
Have your hair washed, your nails manicured,
or your toes painted.

Go On

Find a restaurant to have a cup of coffee,
a glass of tea, soft drink, or water.

Decide

Look at your stress again.
Determine to do something about it.

Repeat

Tackle another stress issue during another
planned two-hour vacation. How does a scented
candlelight bath with soft music sound?

Dear Mom,

Thanks, Mom, for not allowing me to wear high heels in the seventh grade. I now know I had giraffe legs.

Thanks for the banana pudding lessons. I loved your stories about the lady who made meringue to reach the ceiling. I tried to get it there, but never quite made it. Maybe some day. The banana pudding is always good. You make the best.

Thanks for wearing red polish on your toes. It was cool.

Thanks for the extravagantly priced Easter outfits you placed on layaway every year.

Thanks for not allowing me to skimp on piano lessons and for making me continue when I wanted to quit. Thanks for asking me to play "In the Garden" for my piano recital. Through the years it became a favorite.

Thanks for pushing me out of the nest and for the encouragement to go to work. Thanks for the second nudge to get another job when I quit: "No excuse for laziness."

Thanks for all the times you allowed my siblings and me to bring people home who had nowhere to go for Christmas. Thanks for the extra gifts you purchased, which made them feel like a part of our family.

Thanks for taking a leave from your job to stay with me when my husband, Steve, became sick. You took great care of us, and I'll never forget it.

Thanks for believing I could do anything when many times I felt I couldn't. Thanks for loving me all these years.

Love,
Lisa

Chapter

TWO

Mother, May I?
Motherly Interruptions

M Y FRIEND, Sharon, a stay-at-home mom, has two preschool children she enjoys having fun with. One day she cranked up the sound of her stereo as it played Christian music and danced throughout her house. Sharon moved from room to room as she exuberantly sang praises to the Lord. Her toddlers trailed closely behind as they mimicked her movements.

Sharon forgot the insurance man's appointment. With the loud music, she didn't hear him ring the doorbell, nor did she know he heard the music and decided to go around to the back of the house to gain her attention. Sharon reached a crescendo in midair as she imitated a deer's leaping position when she looked to the window and met his wide-eyed stare.

Speechless, Sharon couldn't defend herself. If her children had had the opportunity, they would have said, "Mom isn't crazy. She's having fun."

You may be at wit's end when your four-year-old daughter paints the cat with fingernail polish or your son runs your payroll check through the paper shredder, places worms in your glass of tea, frogs in the toilet, and snakes in a jar under the kitchen sink. Conditions don't improve when he climbs onto the bathroom counter, reaches into the cabinet, and grabs Grandma's heart medication that he swallows. Your nerves may erupt through your fingertips when your preschooler takes a stroll through the neighborhood without telling you or calls 9-1-1 to ask the police to take a look at his train. Stop before you scream. It can be worse.

What if your child is a teenager? It's possible he'll paint his hair blue any day. Or tattoo his chest or pierce his tongue, lip, nose, or navel. He could wreck the car, lose his job, or ask you for a loan you know he'll never repay. What if you've mortgaged your home to send him to college for four years only to have him take a job frying burgers at McDonalds? You say you've already been there?

Then have you sold your insurance policy for a wedding gown, put your best jewelry up for auction on eBay to pay for the flowers, and taken out a twenty-five-year loan for the reception? All of this and in return they present you a grandchild in the form of a cocker spaniel.

20/10 Vision

Before I became a mom, I carefully observed my own mother. I thought she owned 20/10 vision. She saw everything— through it, around it, and over it.

My daily chores as I was growing up included cleaning the kitchen. I was to have this completed before Mom arrived home from work. I got home from school an hour before she did. This was adequate time to complete the chores, but I liked television and my favorite program aired at that hour.

On one particular day, I heard her car as it rolled down the graveled drive. Only so much could be accomplished in thirty seconds. But from much practice, I quickly jumped up, turned off the TV, ran into the kitchen, started the dishwater, and hurriedly cleared the table and counter to make a good first impression.

"Lisa Marie!" I knew the addition of the second name indicated a problem.

Without turning around I said, "Yes, Mom?"

"You just started!"

I turned toward her and gave my best "What do you mean?" look.

With one hand on her hip and the other pointing in my direction, she said, "Don't give me that look. The rocking chair is still moving." It was impossible to fool Mom.

Too Honest?

I've lived away from home for over twenty years. Through the last twelve of them, I've lived in Florida; my mother lives in Virginia. We see one another around four times a year. When we get together, we hold amazingly truthful discussions. This is how it goes.

"I think you weigh more than you ever have."

I look down at my stomach and thighs. Who was I kidding, thinking it was possible to fool her with my oversized shirt? I had to laugh.

"Yes, Mom, I think you're right."

Then we move onto other subjects such as purses.

"I think that is the ugliest purse I've ever seen."

"You don't like my cute black purse with multicolored bows on it?"

"No."

"Mom, it's a very popular brand."

"I don't care. I've always admired your purses, but not this one. Where did you get it? I don't think I want to shop there."

My mother's honesty has always warmed my heart because I know it's a part of her humor—even when she pokes at my pot roast.

This spring she visited us. We had a great time. We shopped. We laughed. We drove. We did everything but cook. Or so I thought. I forgot the roast in the Crock-Pot. It had cooked for fourteen hours. But I thought I'd test it anyway. I couldn't pierce it with a fork. My mother didn't believe the roast could be as bad as I said, so she also made an unsuccessful attempt to stick it.

"Lisa, I know how you enjoy smart shopping, but I don't think you should have settled for less with the meat. Where did you get this thing, the bargain basement?"

Just a glance from my son, Joe, was all it took.

"Did I say something funny?"

In between giggles I said, "Joe and I recently conversed about your candor and this again proves it. We're laughing with you. Mom; we love you."

Teeter-Totter

Mothering is an amazing balancing act. It's like finding our stability on a giant teeter-totter. We're constantly in a dilemma. How do we encourage our children to do their best without making them feel what they've already accomplished isn't good enough? How do we correct these strong willed children without crushing their spirit? How do we present choices for obedience without fostering an environment for rebellion? We're always wondering when enough is too much.

We look to Mary, the mother of Jesus, as we consider the most difficult aspect of parenting. After Jesus was born, Joseph and Mary took him to the temple to present him to the Lord. Simeon prophesied over him.

> Then he blessed them and told Mary, "This child of yours will cause many in Israel to fall and others to stand. The child will be like a warning sign. Many people will reject him, and you, Mary, will suffer as though you had been stabbed with a dagger. But all this will show what people are really thinking" (Luke 2:34, 35 CEV).

This was a tough word for a mother to receive. What if we were told our child would be rejected? Impossible. We envision our child as class valedictorian, state senator, Miss America, Olympic gold medalist, pro football linebacker, Dell Computer CEO, or news anchorman for Fox News. We see ourselves in the best seats at the stadium. We dream of standing behind our child with our hearts pounding loudly as he's sworn into office. We see the camera rolling as we are interviewed afterward by Barbara Walters, who wants to know the secret behind raising an amazing son or daughter. A life of rejection doesn't conform to our well, thought-out plans.

But when we stop to consider the suffering that children cause as they enter the world, this shouldn't come as any surprise. If you've never had a child and you're pregnant, don't spend time around women who've had babies. You don't want to hear their horror stories, especially in a room filled with mothers. Once the stories begin, they grow worse and worse until somebody tops them all.

We're surprised about the whole ordeal. Maybe that's why we're so animated when we share our experience—the absolute shock of it. There are not adequate terms to explain it. But then we wouldn't have believed it anyway.

In the labor room before the pains began, I questioned my mother.

"Why is that woman down the hallway screaming like a bear is attacking her?" Mom gave a sympathetic grin, sort of sighed, and patted my arm.

Natural labor was popular in my community at the time Joe was born—that means no epidurals. In other words, these doctors didn't have a clue what it was like to stand at home plate without a bat for twelve hours unsuccessfully dodging the pitcher's 90 mph fastballs aimed at one's abdomen, side, and back. They'd never passed a baby through an opening the size of a sawed-off flute, nor been cut from stem to stern and made to sit on a water pillow for a year. Then we have this privacy issue. Karen Scalf Linamen shares her experience.

I teach my kids the concept of personal space, and the idea that there are parts of their body that are private. For my daughters, I've described these areas as the parts of the body that would be covered up by a two-piece bathing suit. What I don't tell them is that this definition will apply until they become mothers. Somehow, in the process of conceiving a baby, birthing a baby, and nursing a baby, everything's up for grabs. Between husbands, nurses, doctors, and our newborns, every "private part" we ever had seems to become public property.[1]

When a woman's in labor, she can't be held responsible for anything she says. This is her free pass to say whatever comes to mind. Four years after Joe was born, my sister-in-law, Tammy, decided on the natural deal. She and her husband, Ray, went through the Lamaze trip. They took the classes and practiced the breathing exercises like good little children. On "D" day as Tammy labored to have her first child, Ray dutifully did as he was taught—blew in her face. Finally, sweet, easy-to-get-along-with Tammy had enough and told him to go find somebody else's face to blow in. This is how our children come into the world. It's no hallelujah picnic.

We'd just as soon ignore the 2 a.m. and 6 a.m. feedings—with colic in between. We'd like to believe it's all about seeing the first tooth without the teething. Let's skip over falling down and go straight to the first walk around the park. Forget the fever, constipation, diarrhea, rash, bronchitis, allergies, vomiting, and fits of rage. We want the early morning smiles, giggles, and the sounds of "mama" and "dada." We forge ahead as our lives are sandwiched between the low lows and extreme highs. Even though we'd rather not live with the bad, we can. Our capacity to love is great and miraculously lightens the burden of parental sacrifices. Yet we suffer with the plague of what happens from here.

We don't want to think that our child will be rejected, persecuted for righteousness' sake, or tried with fire. We cringe at the image of our child picking up a cross, fighting the good fight of faith, and laboring to reach his or her goals. Yet this is exactly what the Bible says is required of our sons and daughters. They'll learn humility, obedience, trust, and patience through suffering. Like Mary, we'll stand aside and suffer with our child as if we've been stabbed with a dagger.

When my son, Joe, entered his first year of college, he called to share a conflict with a professor. From hundreds of miles away I listened, my heart hurting with every breath. Finally I said, "Do you want me to go up there and beat the tar out of that man?" We both laughed at the ridiculous picture of his mother beating his professor over the head with her ugly purse. But it hurts. When our children suffer, so do we. Enormously.

Our Heritage

Although we despise the idea of our children suffering, we must be careful not to shield them from all pain. This country was built upon the sweat and blood of many young men and women—children with backbone who knew how to sacrifice. Children who rose at the crack of dawn to work the fields, milk the cows, and feed the pigs.

Jean, a dear friend in her late seventies, invited my husband and me to dinner one evening. She impressed us with stories of her life. Snakes didn't faze her. Why, she climbed under her house with a shotgun and killed a rattler within a few feet from her. We left talking about her strength. I told my husband I fear for the next generation. We're losing something valuable. Tough women like Jean.

I shared this with my prayer partner, Bunny, who responded:

"Lord, raise up women like Jean who will come under the foundations of their home and fight for their families. Women who will take the Word of God and shoot the old devil that's trying to steal them."

We must arise to the need and birth the same desire into our children as we witnessed in our fathers and mothers.

I thank the Lord for the women God empowered through the centuries to turn water into wine, convert passivity into positions of respect, and transformed hardship into a harvest field. Women who redefined submission, liberated captivity, and sprung wide the doors of education. Thank the Lord for his ingenious creativity embedded in the heart of mankind. And for the men who took a wheel and saw a car, saw a bird take flight and said, "One day I will fly too." Men who looked at the moon on a clear summer night and said, "Someday I'm going there."

Thank you, Lord, for the generations who seized the remnant of silk carelessly crumpled in a storage box, and designed ballroom gowns, ties, gloves, and hats fit for royalty. People who saw railroads through western terrain. People who gathered seeds, planted them, nourished them, and watched them grow into a forest.

Young women, we must not curse the morning, despise the dirt, or scorn the heat of the sun. God is calling forth daughters of the pioneer generation. Women who will dig for

> ೦ৎ
>
> Dear woman, this nation was built on your rough and worn hands. We were birthed from your hope in God and nourished from your gardens. We bathed at your wells and warmed at your fires. We embraced the fabric you cut, sewed, scrubbed, and pressed. We must give back to you for your sacrifice. We must not allow your dream to die. We must plant again. Birth again. Harvest again.
>
> ೦ৎ

gold, eat strong meat, travel uneven terrain, and live in dugouts until they reach home—heaven.

I look out the window of my parents' house at the tall pine trees that line the drive. Some have wanted to cut them down. But my heart cries, "No! My daddy planted those trees when I was a little girl. They are over thirty feet tall now."

In this country people are trying to cut away our heritage—to steal what is rightfully ours. They seek to strip away earlier ideas founded on rock-solid principles. They don't want us to extend this salvation to our children.

It's time to work again. Plow the field again. Build again. Sweat again. God is calling forth quilt makers who will take strips of fabric and create a work that will comfort the body of Christ. God is calling forth railroad builders who will bring together communities of people for the next generation. God is calling you and God is calling me. This is the Joshua day where we will walk in the actualization of the dream. We must not fail.

Pioneers are not called to fame but to a future. They are not called to the podium but to the pit. They are not called to be admired but to adversity. We must present this to our children.

Mama Bird

As I continued to ponder along the lines of suffering and our children, I believe God revealed something to me as I prayed. It was as if I had seen a mama bird sitting on a nest, her eggs hatched and her fledglings were ready to fly. Instead of obeying instinct and shoving her children out of the nest, the mama bird succumbed to fear. Instead of trusting God to take care of her babies, she felt she was the only one who could provide for them. While she sat on the nest, her babies became fatter and fatter.

We're sitting on the nest when we fight our children's battles for them. We can't always be there to cover for them. Our children are still in the nest when we allow them to sleep the day away and don't teach them responsibility by giving them household chores. Our children must experience good feelings associated with accomplishing tasks. We're not preparing our children for life by paying for their car, clothes, and college. Our children need to learn to work. They need to learn early in life the difference between right and wrong. I like what Arkansas Governor Mike Huckabee says:

> When a pilot flies into a city, he encounters miles of concrete in all directions; but it is crucial that the pilot land only on a particular strip of concrete to which the air traffic controller directs him. If he lands on the freeway in

rush-hour traffic, hundreds of people could die. Is it narrow-minded to limit him to that one strip of concrete? Perhaps so, but anything else leads to disaster.

Our children must be told which concrete is safe to land on. Too often we fail to say, "This is right; anything else is wrong." Instead we say, "Wherever you want to go is fine." There are a lot of places in Little Rock where there's room to land a jetliner, and most of them are wrong.[2]

During kindergarten, my son's class was required to wear clothes like a popular rock star and sing his song during a school musical. This particular star was involved in the occult and a number of other blatant sins, and I couldn't allow my son to imitate him. This was to be a fun day for Joe and his class. We didn't want to foster an environment for future rebellion. So we, as parents, presented him with another choice. I talked to the teacher, not condemning her, but explaining our position. Steve and I talked to Joe and offered him a better choice—the zoo. We had a great day.

When Joe was in first grade, several violent cartoons were popular. Rather than expose him to these shows, I rose early and videotaped several Christian cartoons for him to view when he came home from school. These cartoons were age appropriate and presented him with agreeable choices for good versus evil. He liked the arrangement. It was a good compromise.

Later, like many others his age, my son wanted to hang out at the mall with his friends when he was about ten years old. I felt uncomfortable with this request for several reasons. This environment lacked adult supervision. I was uncertain about the other children participating in this venture. I didn't know if he'd encounter negative peer pressure that he'd be spiritually mature enough to combat. We can't take unnecessary chances with our children by exposing them to potentially dangerous situations. Because I didn't like this arrangement, I said no, but I presented him with a fun alternative.

I've protected my child as any good parent would, as I'm certain you have. When are we being overly concerned for our child's safety—physically, emotionally, and spiritually? Some children never spend the night with a friend, never attend church-sponsored camps, never make friends, and never attend children's church or Sunday school. Some children never know their grandparents, aunts, or uncles—some for good reason while others are simply denied this privilege because the parent is overprotective.

Some boys are not allowed to play sports for fear they'll be hurt. Where's the father in this situation? The mother overrules him. She demands and he submits to her demands. Some children never play with the neighborhood children, for fear they'll be wrongly influenced. But this isn't our only block to stumble over.

We live in a materialistic society. Our children are pressured at every turn to keep up with their peers. We're afraid to deny them. We give and give, and we don't know how to jump off this roller coaster without harm. We give too soon. Some children have nothing to wait for—not even sex.

What a thrill it was to finally receive permission to have my ears pierced. I didn't have to glue BBs to them anymore. I thought the day would never arrive when I could wear high heels and panty hose, shave my legs, and fit my AAs into a bra.

I wonder if Sarah thought Isaac was worth the wait, if Hannah thought Samuel worth the wait, if the prophetess

Anna thought Jesus worth the wait, and if the disciples thought the Holy Spirit worth the wait.

Codependency

Another reason why we find it difficult to release our children is codependency. It's as if the umbilical cord is still attached between mother and child. When that is the case, we can't operate independently from our child and our child can't function independently from us.

A codependent child doesn't bond well with his or her peers when the child is too attached to a parent. Even though the parent doesn't desire all the baggage that surrounds a codependent relationship, the mom or dad feeds on the child's need for the parent.

Many times, the pattern is traced back many generations. The relationship appears healthy; the family may be regarded as being close. But the results are tragic because as the child grows older and marries, she finds it difficult to emotionally leave home. Many times, the grown child's husband has difficulty with this family tie. He succumbs to it, violently resists it, or attempts persuasive arguments against it.

What should happen? From the moment a child is born and the umbilical cord is broken, the child should learn to survive outside of the mother's womb, learn to receive nourishment outside the womb, learn to sleep on their own, and learn to walk away from the mother. This can be difficult for the mother. She doesn't want her child to do well without her. The mother wants her child to need her embrace as much as the mother needs the child's embrace. She continues to force the attachment when the child naturally pulls away. The child reaches for independence while the mother wants her dependence. But the parent has to fight this urge and let them go—they can't be the child's entire world.

Life is a series of letting go. Drs. Cloud and Townsend believe every parent needs to learn to let their kids go.

> Parenting is the only relationship God designed whose goal is that it ends. That is why, in a sense, if you are a good parent, you are headed for heartbreak. You spend years loving, training, denying yourself, and sacrificing for your children, and in return they move away from you.[3]

I planned for my son to leave home. Two years before he left for school, I ceased doing his laundry. He also learned to cook, and to manage money through working at a local grocery store. When it was time for him to leave for college, we loaded his provisions and took him to his dorm. We spent a few days there to ensure he was settled, but then when the time came to leave, I got into the car and drove away. I left him. I cried most of the way home. But I left him. I didn't call him every day. I left him.

Eventually, I had to find a way of trusting God with Joe. I prayed, "Lord, I've done all I know to do as a mother. I give the rest to you to do as you wish." Every day, I pray that he will find and pursue his God-ordained purpose and not leave this earth until he fulfills it. Throughout his life I've prayed for God to bring a special woman to assist him—and he to assist her—in fulfilling God's purpose.

I pray daily that he will love God with all of his heart, mind, soul, and strength. I pray that he will not be deceived and that God will protect him from all harm. Every time I pray I release him to God a little more. At times I've even lifted my hands to God and said, "God, take my mess and do something with it if you can."

Repentance

As parents, eventually we discover that even with our best effort, we're not all knowing. We're maturing alongside our children. In our immaturity, we mistakenly offer bad advice and criticism when comfort is most needed. We discover our time isn't always well spent and our focus may be gravely misdirected. Oftentimes, our failure doesn't greet us for many years. These revelations tend to defeat us. We fail to realize much worse can happen than occasionally missing the mark as parents. The worst part is refusing to repent to God and our children when our misdemeanor appears. I've returned to Joe on several occasions and expressed sorrow for messing up as a parent.

We can't expect our child to know by osmosis that we're sorry for past failures. It's important we communicate our failures to our children. Without this vital information, they grow up with the wrong impressions. They fail to understand our heart. They reject the truth that we care if we fail to communicate the truth.

I once attended a seminar about the development of intimate relationships. During one of these classes, I became deeply convicted regarding the manner I handled a situation three years earlier. Joe had goofed off in school during a critical time where scholarship opportunities were offered. I was angry and blew up. I failed to notice his struggles in adapting to another new school—his eighth. While he wasn't exempt from responsibility, I was accountable for my handling of the situation.

In the few days following the seminar, I sought the right opportunity to speak to Joe. When it came, I explained my failure by placing my need for him to receive a scholarship above his need for understanding. I expressed deep remorse for this failure, and didn't attempt to make excuses. After I finished my apology, he said, "Have you been to another one of those seminars?" We laughed a little tearfully.

If we fail to apologize to our children, we fail to offer healing for words spoken or actions taken that may have critically wounded them. I know a mother who accused her twelve-year-old daughter of separating the mother from the father. These words were spoken in anger and reinforced a lie the child already believed. I shiver when I consider the damage this mother forced upon her child and the apology that may never be forthcoming or received.

Repentance is one of the most important aspects of parenting. We must be receptive of God's correction. Even at this, wounds we inflict on our children can take many years to resolve. Yet, we mustn't forget that the resolution begins with our admission that we're wrong.

The Future

We slough off our frustration over our children's misdemeanors with all sorts of funnies, but without exception our children make us proud. We believe our little darling is beautiful—

whether toothless, cone-headed, pumpkin-shaped, or freckled-faced. Our child doesn't have to be the smartest in the class or the most athletic or a creative whiz or a gifted communicator. We believe in him or her.

We want a guarantee that our children will never stray. Will they make my same mistakes? Will they learn from my instructions? Has he listened—has she heard my heart?

In our turmoil we lose sight of the fact that God loves our children more than we do. We're privileged to raise them and love them, but ultimately they belong to God and we must surrender their failures and their successes to him. When I partner with God in parenting, there is no fear for the future, for he holds the future. I give it to him to do whatever he pleases.

I Can Do Something About This

I can do everything through him who gives me strength
(Philippians 4:3)

Pray

Dearest Lord,
I am attempting to make right choices for my child and to give
him space to make choices. I can't say I've never failed you in this
parenting process. In looking back, I know I'd do things differently.
I repent of my wrongdoing. I'll not carry it, for it's been released
to you. _____ belongs to you. I renounce the curse
of sin, for blessings belong to us. I embrace faith rather than fear.
I hope in you always. For I know your will is that my child
will prosper. I trust you with the future.

Search

Do I need to repent?

Write

What do I need to repent of?

Share

Talk to your child about this.

Determine

Decide to develop stronger communication with your child.

Make

Make an appointment with your child
every week to have fun and to share.

And in despair I bowed my head;
"There is no peace on earth," I said;
"For hate is strong,
And mocks the song
Of peace on earth, goodwill to men!"

Then pealed the bells more loud and deep:
"God is not dead; nor doth he sleep!
The wrong shall fail,
The right prevail,
With peace on earth, goodwill to men!"

—HENRY WADSWORTH LONGFELLOW[1]

Chapter
THREE

It's Not Fair!
Undeserved Interruptions

S OCIAL INJUSTICE abounds. Ask Chris Matthews, Rush Limbaugh, Bill O'Reilly, or Larry King. Save the manatee! Hug a tree! Right to life! Stop war! Health care! Prescription drugs! Government waste! NAACP! NOW! MADD! ACLU! They debate, demonstrate, terminate, stagnate, interrogate, and frustrate until some are senseless with rage. Do they have a cause? Certainly! Do they have rights? Unquestionably!

It's unfair when senior adults who survive on a limited income have to pay large prescription drug prices. It's unfair when many feel trapped in the health insurance crisis. It's unfair when innocent babies die unprotected. It's unfair when children suffer abandonment. It's unfair when our lives are controlled with unnecessary laws. It's unfair when the Supreme Court overrides the state. It's unfair when a drunken driver kills a child.

It's unfair when men rape women, a teacher is murdered, a friend persecuted, a co-worker robbed, or a mother beaten. It's unfair to be slandered and humiliated. It's unfair when justice is withheld and the guilty go unpunished.

It's unfair when a president receives blame for the former administration's decisions. It's unfair to lose a job as a result of the economy. It's unfair to be wrongly sued and then to be ordered to pay the legal fees. It's unfair to be discriminated against because of age, gender, or race. It's unfair to continually forgive an alcoholic abusive husband.

And we're outraged by unfairness to our children. We hate violence on television and pornography on the Internet. We're disgusted when teachers tell our children it's okay to be homosexual, it's okay to have sex, it's okay to abort babies, it's okay to disobey parents.

We're tired of people who tell us what we can't do:

"You can't pray!"

"You can't discipline your child!"

"You can't read your Bible!"

"You can't mention Jesus!"

Life's unfairness doesn't always slap us in the face with big issues. Sometimes it's only a mother or wife who fixes all the meals, bakes the cookies, washes the clothes, presses the shirts, yet experiences little if any appreciation.

Life at times just isn't fair, is it?

Born into Unfairness

We're born into an unfair world. As children we cried, "That's not fair!" as we stomped our feet, slammed the door, and slumped onto the floor. Our indignation arose from unfair judgments from our parents or mistreatment from a sibling or an undeserved school grade or a cruel remark gossiped by a trusted friend or a sickness that prevented us from playing outside. We've all suffered the harshness of growing up in a world that is extremely unfair—where the top achiever is often overlooked and the slacker occasionally receives the prize.

We expected our parents to possess yardstick memories, pinpoint insight, and tape-measure oversight as wide and deep as the circumstance. Oftentimes, life wasn't fair because parents didn't understand our needs—our need of candy before lunch . . . bedtime at midnight . . . playtime, all the time . . . and I must always win.

Yet, along with childish expectations over what is fair come the more confusing ones. Why do some children eat imported crab for dinner while others scour trash bins for discarded bread? Why do some cuddle with loving parents while others fear their next attack? Why do some dream, laugh, and hope while others nightmare, weep, and dread? Why do some know blessings while others know curses? Why are some born into a society who knows Jesus while others never know Sunday school, never hear Billy Graham, or never meet a Christian?

Children suffer when the world is upside down.

When Robert pastored in Jacksonville, Florida, an attractive couple from our church discovered she was pregnant. The family and church members rejoiced with them. We presented her with a baby shower and anticipated the arrival of their daughter. On the day of delivery we received the heartbreaking news that the baby had a rare disease, resulting in severe internal complications and a deformed face.

Little Danielle survived the first few weeks and the doctors eventually determined that with numerous surgeries throughout her lifetime she would overcome her ailments and have a relatively normal life. Danielle quickly won our hearts with her smile. She seemed to be a divine miracle in progress.

But then one day when two years old, Danielle went to the dentist to have a minor problem corrected. She panicked and it caused a restriction of oxygen flow through her abnormally small esophagus, which caused her heart to fail. They could not revive her, and Danielle died. Her death left us all knowing she was born into an unfair world under conditions neither she nor her family would have chosen.

Personal Unfairness

When a neighbor's heart is set against us, it just doesn't seem fair. Regardless of our kindness to this person, she resents us. If we send a card, she says we're doing it out of duty. If we offer a gift, she fails to notice the love behind it. If we make our way toward her, she quickly turns to avoid us. If we call, she refuses to answer. Her heart is against us.

She searches our every word for flaws she can use against us. If we confront the situation, she says it's our imagination and our sensitivity. She secretly carries her accusations to her friends in the form of prayer requests. Her heart is against us and it hurts. With all our resources, we attempt to change what we don't understand. We want to shout, "If you took the chance to know me, I think you'd like me." We despise the division. We want her to like us. But remorse eventually turns to anger.

"Hey, lady! I'm sorry I stepped on your big toe. I really didn't mean to. I have awfully big feet and I'm a bit clumsy. Don't you understand what it means to be s-o-r-r-y?"

Silence.

"Okay, you want to be like that? Have it your way! I don't need you. I don't need your garbage in my kitchen while I'm cooking." We slam the door and start a new project—one a little safer.

When life isn't fair, it consumes our thinking. We can't think of anything but the terrible deed. Our day may be filled with a heavy agenda of two committee meetings, four employee interviews, a conference call, a luncheon appointment, and a parent-teacher conversation. Because our schedule is driven, we feel we've forgotten the unfair situation. But when we stop for coffee, it comes back. We walk into the bathroom and look into the mirror. It comes back. We step into our car and drive to the teacher meeting. It comes back.

Our child says, "Earth to Mom." We're thinking about it. We're cooking dinner, thinking about it. We're having devotions with our children, thinking about it. We go to bed, wondering what we have to do to quit thinking about it. Why can't we stop?

Our stomach twists into pieces. We feel we've eaten a bag of salted chips without water. We don't remember where we parked the car. Our nerves feel as if they're exposed and projected outward from every limb. Then a woman with all the answers offers advice. She has the audacity to counsel when she hasn't once cried with us.

Why are we so angry when life isn't fair? Do we think somebody is getting by with something? Has the injustice slipped past totally unnoticed?

Our insatiable thirst for justice must be satisfied without delay. After all in the movies, within two hours, the bad guy is pierced with a four-foot sword and pressed between six metal rollers. If this didn't kill him, he's then thrown through an enlarged window from a thirty-nine-story office building.

God never stops. He interrupts our afternoon nap. He whispers in our ear as we're driving to the shopping mall. He reminds us through a passage in a book. He knows we can't be effective with this attitude. Just as much as he wants to help her, he wants to help us.

Pray for her.

We say, "I can't pray for her. You'll probably make me hug her. Or worse yet, tell her it's my fault. I've been there before with her. I don't want to do this anymore. I want my life to go on."

Pray for her.

Yes, I encountered a similar situation. I prayed without ceasing for this woman. Oftentimes, her attitude angered me. I pounded my hands on the floor and shouted my prayers at God. I cried uncontrollably because I hated the terrible division.

"Lord, I desperately need your help. I choose to forgive her for slandering my name. I choose to bless her. I choose to love her. I choose to allow your will to be done. I refuse to allow her to steal my joy."

One day I said, "Lord I have done everything you have asked me to do. I've called her, prayed without ceasing, extended every kindness, and repeatedly walked across the church foyer to have my warmth returned with coldness. I don't know why nothing has changed."

As I rode in the passenger seat next to my husband on our way to a dinner party, these words came to me: *Lisa, be at peace because you have obeyed me in every request I made of you concerning her. You've done your part. You can't make this happen. Leave the results to me.* I did.

In the following months, I watched a miracle unfold. A strange thing happened. We were paired to work on a project from which neither of us could gracefully remove ourselves. I became physically ill with every meeting because of the awkwardness of the situation. Yet, I continued to go.

During one of these meetings, she reached over and handed me something she made. I knew this was her way of saying, "Everything is OK, but don't make a fuss." I warmly thanked her and cried all the way home. I knew a miracle occurred.

Today we share a rare love for one another. I treasure her simple gift as if it were priceless gold. This gift reminds me to never cease praying, to never cease doing right, to never stop trusting God when I'm treated unfairly.

Yet, I'm aware all stories do not have a happy earthly ending.

I have a dear friend who was treated in the cruelest manner. On many occasions I wept for her. During one of my powwows with God I said, "Lord, judge these people right now!" Immediately I sensed His rebuke.

Don't ask for judgment unless you're ready for judgment yourself. Pray for my mercy.

History Book's List of Unfairness

Unfairness has existed since the earliest date in history. No one has ever been exempt from unfair treatment—not even God's chosen. It began when Abel was thrown into a hole in the ground and continued with Joseph thrown into slavery. We shouldn't have been surprised when Shadrach, Meshach, and Abednego were thrown into a furnace, Daniel thrown into a lion's den, Jeremiah thrown into a cistern, John the Baptist thrown under the sword, and Paul and Silas thrown into prison.

Just as it was unfair for men so it was with women of every nationality and walk of life. A woman didn't own property; she was property. A woman didn't have rights; she was every man's right. A woman didn't possess freedom; she was enslaved by another's freedom. She was the concubine, foreigner, widow. She was the woman with an issue of blood, the woman holding an alabaster box, the Samaritan woman, the adulteress woman, the woman without a name.

We struggle with the unfairness of God's elite who suffered greatly before death. According to historical tradition, the disciple Thomas was tortured by angry pagans, run through with spears, and thrown into the flames of an oven. Matthew was nailed to the ground with spikes and beheaded. James, Jesus' own half brother, was cast from the temple tower, and then beaten with a club until he died. Matthias, who replaced Judas, was stoned and then beheaded. Peter was crucified upside down at his request. And John was boiled in oil but wasn't hurt, so he was banned to the Island of Patmos where he received the Book of Revelation.[2]

The *World Christian Encyclopedia* reports that at a steady rate over the last twenty centuries seventy million Christians, in 238 countries, have been martyred for Christ.[3]

Life isn't fair. We know it's true because the Bible declares it. God doesn't explain why we've been mistreated. Oftentimes, he's silent about the whole affair. God never explained to Job why he lost everything, why he suffered, why his friends accused him.

Sometimes we spend our lives saying we'll serve God as long as he treats us well, but if he fails us—we're out of here. With this type of theology, if we were Job, we'd fail the test. If we were Abraham and asked to sacrifice our son, we'd fail the test. If we were Joseph, thrown into a pit and sold into slavery, no doubt we would fail the test. If we were John on the Island of Patmos, after witnessing the deaths of our dearest friends, we'd fail the test.

What Can I Do?

Every time we say "I can't," we also say "I can" to something else:

I can't trust, but I can despair.
I can't forgive, but I can hate.
I can't pray, but I can gossip.
I can't obey, but I can worry.
I can't go, but I can stay.
I can't love, but I can fear.
I can't work, but I can sit.

Whole worlds of "I cannots" are ready to present themselves to us. But what *can* one person do?

I can stop thinking about the unjust interruption in my life. I can determine to move beyond this point. I can remind myself with a note on my refrigerator that I do not have to stay here. I can set my mind to better days. I can forgive. I can trust God. I can be healed. I can help others. I can laugh again.

I can stop channel-surfing past hungry children and take some of the money I use to pack my freezer to feed them instead. I can be a shoulder for a friend to cry on. I can plant a tree in memory of my child. I can be a Big Sister. I can volunteer at the hospital. I can write my state representative, write an editor, write a government agency.

My mother worked in a cotton mill from the time she was sixteen. She worked under cruel conditions. The temperatures exceeded a hundred degrees. Perspiration provided a good adhesive for cotton to cling to—from every exposed body part. The windows were kept shut tight because of the concern that a draft would hinder production. The workers ate on overturned trashcans in the bathroom. They endured long hours without breaks. Through the years, my mother wrote letters to her superintendent, the company president, and the U.S. Occupational Safety and Health Administration, all of whom responded. Gradually, the conditions became better. Her determination, along with others, paved the way for a better working environment for many young workers today. She did something about unfairness. Before she retired, she found the mill an enjoyable place to work.

What if she had never said a word? What if she had waited for somebody more educated, more experienced, more articulate, more charismatic to speak up? If everyone thought the Christian community was called to passivity, a woman wouldn't own land, vote, or receive employment benefits equal to those of a man. We are a voice for the destitute.

We're interrupted with falsehoods at every corner. We're obligated to speak the truth in the midst of this injustice. We're obligated to gently lead the way in trusting God. Let's be the ones who first receive healing so we can then disperse healing.

We confuse a strong voice with unrighteous anger. We associate human rights with wrongs when the issue is not entirely about rights but also about purpose. What bars the door to the fulfillment of our purpose? Are we not called to be bold? We define turning the other cheek as waiting on the Lord. Are we waiting on the Lord, or are we too tired to fight? If my friend is in prison for the sake of the gospel, I refuse to leave her to decay. I'm not in prison, therefore, I'm obligated to use my liberty to free her. She's called to fulfill her purpose in Christ. I must see she does. I must be a voice for God.

We have a voice. How do we use it? We speak the truth in love. We plead for the widow, the orphaned, the poor, and the lost. We petition God on their behalf. We pray for laborers to enter the harvest. We encourage women to become involved. We work while we can. The happiest people I know are those who are busy loving others.

Trust God

Although I've said "trust God," I don't think it's all that simple. Trusting God can't be suddenly conjured up in the midst of a crisis. Trust is what we do *before* the avalanche. To scramble around for trust when we're covered with a mountain of debris is a difficult task. How do we trust God if we've never developed a lifestyle of trust? It's not impossible to slowly gain trust when we're in turmoil, but it's difficult.

Trust knows daylight is merely a few hours past nightfall. Trust answers when the valley of death knocks. Trust twirls in peace through windy seas. Trust treads the desert expecting to find a water fountain. Trust outwits the serpent, outlasts the storm, outweighs the loss, outlives the fire, outlaws the devil. Trust keeps what others discard—a broken life. Trust always believes there's hope.

Some want to remove "in God we trust" from our currency. They don't know the God of our early founding fathers. They haven't felt His hand in times of war. They haven't listened for his voice when constitutional counsel was sought. They haven't birthed a nation with the greatness of the Almighty beside them. They've denied the hand extended toward them, they've discounted the truth, and they've turned toward turmoil. They survive without God.

They trust what they hold in their hands. They trust what their eyes tell them. They trust what others say. They trust science and medicine. They trust chariots and horses. They trust in an ocean that will never part. They trust in a wall that will never crumble. They trust in a desert that will never bring forth water. They trust in a giant that will never slay their enemy. They trust in an altar that will never produce fire. They trust in an idol that will never feed them. They trust in a war that will never offer peace. Not so with those who place their trust in God.

How do I explain the joy in my heart when I'm at my lowest? How do I explain the peace I feel when life doesn't look good? How do I explain the voice that speaks to me when no one is around? How do I share the love that I experience when encountering an enemy? How do I say God is my friend when he can't be seen?

I trust in a voice as silent as a tissue falling to the ground. I trust in a hand that moves when we're looking the other way. I trust in miracles we can't trace. I trust in words written long ago. I trust in outrageous acts of heroism. I trust in a resurrection, a cross, a love, a God-Man. I trust what I cannot fully grasp, what others don't believe, what I can't explain, what I refuse to recount. Some call me crazy. God calls me blessed.

God Twists Unfairness

God has an amazing way of circumnavigating an unfair situation to our benefit. He took me, a hyperactive adult, and placed me in a closet-like hospital room for four and a half weeks in St. Louis. The drapes were closed and the room was very dark—due to my husband's illness. Because of the isolated environment, I could exit the room only for one hour a day.

God knew what he was doing. Here I am sixteen years later staring at a computer for endless hours. The walls seem a little closet-like sometimes; other times, I feel I'm six feet underground, digging my way to air. But I had to go St. Louis before I could be here. Because I went there, I'm doing much better here. God twists our situations around when we allow it.

I confided my unfair situation to a dear friend and counselor, Larry Gillespie. He responded with these wise words, "Lisa, find meaning in the suffering."

His statement landed in a soft place and has since cushioned me in areas of crisis. When a crisis strikes, I immediately pray for God to reveal the ways by which I benefit from it. I know if the benefit is found, I'll make it. Then the suffering isn't in vain.

For every tear shed, may an ocean of love spring forth for others.
With every sleepless night, may there be endless days to cheer a friend.
May this persecution prove God's love. May my loss be another's gain.
May the ending be a beginning of renewed faith.
May I become nothing so God can become something.
May my sorrow birth freedom.
May my despair deliver hope.
May my barrenness produce fruit.
May today pave the way for a better tomorrow.

The Greatest Act of Unfairness

Jesus never denied the existence of unfairness. He said we'd encounter enemies, be persecuted, and walk among hypocrites. We'd like to think Jesus is mistaken. We want to believe that someday the hypocrite will disappear, our enemy will find somebody else to torment, and we'll no longer be persecuted. We're tired of one battle after another. We hate living in a world that believes a lie.

"I did it my way! The greatest love is me. My body is my own and I can do whatever I want to with it. You're a right-wing extremist! I have a right to be gay, but you don't have a right to pray."

Some cry over the injustice of being born with many disadvantages. They feel they can never reach the other side because of their poor start. Don't forget how far Jesus fell. The Son of God soared from heaven and landed into a ravaged, unfair world. Not only did Jesus choose to come here, but he also consented to stay for thirty-three years. Do we know of a thief, liar, child sex offender, drug addict, alcoholic, wife beater, arsonist, male chauvinist, whiner, or hypochondriac we'd like to be shacked up with for thirty-three years? No wonder Jesus fought so hard to pray.

The sin of humankind didn't stop Jesus from coming to earth. Nor did wickedness stop him from healing a blind or lame or leprous man. Lack of preparation by others didn't prevent him from turning the water to wine; a death sentence didn't prevent him from raising the dead; the spiritual blindness of others didn't prevent him from correcting bad doctrinal issues; and the willfulness of others didn't prevent him from delivering the demon possessed.

Jesus came to die for people who didn't care and who wouldn't receive him as their Savior. The greatest act of injustice ever done to a human being came in the form of a cross.

It was unfair for an innocent man to die. It was unfair for the Son of God to be persecuted, slandered, and murdered. It was unfair for him to take my place. It was unfair for him to do it alone. But because he did, I am free.

Not free from unfairness. Not free from danger. Not free from persecution. Not free from death. But free to die. Free to live. Free to forgive. Free to trust. Free to love. Free to surrender. Free to hope. Free to choose.

Jesus, our great intercessor, will weep with you in your loneliness. He's been lonely. Jesus will comfort your distress. He's suffered distress. Jesus will defend you. He's been defenseless. Jesus offers peace in exchange of turmoil, hope for dead-end streets, laughter to replace tears, and a brighter day than you've ever known.

Jesus takes the unfairness that's worked against you for many years and makes it work on your behalf. The entrance into this grand and glorious help is through the keyword discussed earlier—TRUST.

With every act of unfairness comes the freedom to choose. Your biggest mistake may be that you believe all of your choices have been stripped from you. Oh, you might not be able to retrieve your lost job, lost marriage, lost home, lost children, lost purse, or lost reputation, but you can surrender it to the one who can. You can take all of life's unfairness, place it on a platter, and give it to Jesus—the one who understands unfairness more than anyone else.

"Though he slay me, yet will I hope in him" (Job 13:15).

I Can Do Something About This

I can do everything through him who gives me strength
(Philippians 4:3)

Pray
Dearest Lord,
Sometimes I'm overwhelmed when life becomes unfair.
I feel my kindness has been taken advantage of. I don't want
to become an angry, bitter person, nor do I want to slander
others. Please help me to forgive when necessary and to
receive your strength. I want to be an example of Christianity
and for the love of Jesus to shine forth in my life.

Draw
Draw a picture of how unfair situations make you feel.

Are there any people in this picture?

Words
What words come to mind when you think of this
unfairness? Write them down in various colors,
shapes, and sizes on your drawing.

Circle
Circle the words that speak most loudly to you.

Confess
Look at the words and ask,
"Do I need to forgive anybody?
Do I need emotional healing?"

Draw

Create another picture telling how you want to feel.

Words

Write words describing how you feel in this picture.

Plan

What can you do to help yourself feel these positive emotions?

When earth's last picture is painted, and the tubes
are twisted and dried.
When the oldest colors have faded, and the
youngest critic has died,
We shall rest, and, faith we shall need it—lie down
for an aeon or two.
Till the Master of All Good Workmen shall set us
to work anew.

—RUDYARD KIPLING[1]

Chapter
FOUR

❧❧

I Quit!
Resigning Interruptions

❧❧

I'M TIRED of making beds, folding laundry, cooking dinner, scrubbing tubs, washing dishes, cleaning floors. I'm tired of screaming kids, a husband who's always late, of being taken for granted. I quit!"

Her husband and children run after her. "But Mama, you can't quit! Who'll take care of us?" She keeps going, not looking back.

Mothers do that? More often than we think.

In another state, Gloria walks into the office, marches directly to her supervisor and slams her hands down onto his desk.

"I'm tired of working Saturdays. I'm tired of promised promotions I never receive. I'm tired of disrespect. I'm tired of your refusal to return my calls. I'm tired of crummy insurance, poor retirement benefits, and low investment opportunities. I quit!"

Heard by a mother as she stood outside the door of her teenage daughter's room: "I can't make good grades. School is boring. The peer pressure is overwhelming. The teachers are prejudiced. I'll marry a rich man. I quit!"

In the hospital cafeteria when Janet was asked about her diet, she said, "Losing weight is too difficult. I don't have the will to battle this anymore. I'm destined to be a large woman. After all, my mother is big. My aunts and grandmother are all obese. It runs in the genes. This is a no-win situation. I quit!"

As Georgia walked into the church parking lot, she was heard muttering, "This place is full of hypocrites. All they want is money. The people aren't friendly. The pastor doesn't preach in the style I'm accustomed to. It's my only day to rest. I'll stay home and watch church on television. I quit!"

One would think they collaborated and decided today was the day to quit. Daily we hear these reports and daily we deal with the results of quitting. Charles Swindoll warns us about a quitting mentality.

> I fear our generation has come dangerously near the "I'm-getting-tired-so-let's-just-quit" mentality. And not just in the spiritual realm. Dieting is a discipline, so we stay fat. Finishing school is a hassle, so we bail out. Cultivating a close relationship is painful, so we back off. Getting a book written is demanding, so we stop short. Working through conflicts in a marriage is a tiring struggle, so we walk away.

Sticking with an occupation is tough, so we start looking elsewhere . . . And about the time we are ready to give up, along comes the Master, who leans over and whispers: "Now keep going; don't quit. Keep on."[2]

As we sat in the neurosurgeon's office, he explained the situation that lay behind my husband's ruptured spinal disk.

"Steve, it isn't necessarily what recently occurred that caused the problem. It's the accumulation of stress you've placed on your back all these years. You could have reached down to retrieve a dropped pencil and suddenly felt pain from a turned disk."

This same idea applies to everyday living. The overload is the last drop poured into the cup that causes the coffee to spill over into the saucer. Maybe it's a negative comment carelessly spoken by a well-meaning friend. Or dirty towels on the bathroom floor or ants in the kitchen or dusty furniture. What about office work on your day off, a phone call asking for a favor, a sick child, an elderly parent, an empty refrigerator, bills to pay? It could be your spouse merely asking you to pour a second glass of tea at the dinner table.

Something snaps inside, and we explode. A voice whispers, "This situation will never change. We don't have to take it anymore. Just leave. Nobody cares."

We quit because we think we're fresh out of choices. We think the bad guy is winning and God's on vacation. We think the murderer who got off the hook because of legal technicalities will never be held accountable for his crime. We quit because our fear is greater than our faith. We quit because we believe obedience is too high a price. Maybe we quit because we believe God doesn't know how to handle the situation. Maybe we think we deserve better. Maybe we believe we're destined for failure. Maybe our perspective is wrong.

Something Happens When We Quit

When we quit we gain a temporary reprieve, but settle for ultimate destruction. When we quit our job before finding a new one, we suffer financial loss. When we quit our marriage before learning to solve problems, we carry problems into a new marriage. When we quit controlling our weight, we inherit a health crisis. When we quit mortgage payments, we forfeit our home. When we quit weeding our garden, the vegetables die. When we quit believing in God, we settle for less. Something happens when we quit.

Marilyn couldn't forgive her mother for abandoning her as a child. She was determined to be a good mother and wife. She adored her children and lavished them with love and attention—until she met another man. Then she abandoned them and her husband, just as her mother had done.

This new man eventually left his wife and children to marry Marilyn. But after a few years, he decided to return to his former wife. Now Marilyn's children hate her, and she is destitute. Quitting never solves problems.

Once we quit the first time, we're easily tempted to quit a second time. When the job is too difficult, we quit again and again until the job reference section on our resume consumes three pages. When we have walked out of our first marriage, it's much easier to walk out of the second.

The discouragement of being a quitter hovers over us like a plague for the rest of our lives. Quitting evokes feelings of failure. We are less likely to try again. As our challenges diminish, we settle for less until eventually we're on the bottom. An excellent speaker becomes a taxi driver. A corporate secretary waits tables. A doctor finds himself living on the street. A housewife and mother turns to prostitution.

Jonah quit his job because he didn't like the way God did business. God wanted Jonah to go to Nineveh, the capital of Assyria, and preach a message of salvation. The Assyrians were known for inhumane treatment of their prisoners. Some had their abdomens sliced, and then a live cat was placed inside. After the prisoner's abdomen was restitched, the Assyrians watched the cat claw its way out. They slung Israelite infants against the wall and even ripped open pregnant women. Jonah understandably had more than a small problem with the Assyrians.

Jonah struggled to obey a God who extended mercy to cruel people. But before we become too hardened against Jonah, we must consider his dilemma and ask ourselves how we'd feel if we witnessed these atrocities. What if it was our grandchild slaughtered, our parents desecrated, or our sister violated?

Like Jonah, I've watched God promote people I didn't think deserved elevation. I've witnessed God bless my enemy without my permission. Eventually, I came to terms with the situation and stopped fighting God in areas I knew nothing about. Oh, I thought I knew it all, but I didn't. I've had to remind myself—*I see only to the bend in the road and no more.*

God didn't need Jonah, an unwilling participant; he could have employed someone else. Why force him into submission? I'm convinced God hated seeing Jonah wallow in his shallow perspective. He yearned to take Jonah to a higher level. Jonah needed God just as much as the Ninevites did. He needed to know him as the God of mercy, and the Israelite nation needed to know this too.

We all suffer when someone quits. Innocent children suffer when their parents quit trying. Restaurant guests suffer when the chef walks out. Church congregations suffer when the pastor leaves town. Parents suffer when their children commit suicide.

What if Sarah had quit and Isaac had never been born? Or Hannah had quit and Samuel hadn't been born? What if Jochebed succumbed to Pharoah's oppression and surrendered Moses? And others suffer when we quit. The whole nation of Assyria, including precious little girls and boys, would have suffered with Jonah's failure. They would have missed an important lesson on the mercy of God, a lesson from which we all benefit.

Drs. Cloud and Townsend tell us to focus on getting *through* the difficulty rather than on getting *out*.

> Whether the problem relates to career, relationships, health, emotions, or loss, we all tend to focus our energies on putting out the fire and making sure it doesn't flare up again soon. . . . It's a problem, it's painful, and you want it gone. So that's what you concentrate on.
>
> There's nothing wrong with trying to solve the problem and alleviate the pain. But the way out of our problems shouldn't be our first concern because God sees our difficulties very differently than we do.
>
> The word *through* is important here, for God is not as concerned with getting us out of problems as he is in getting us through problems.[3]

I quit writing, one time, due to feelings of inferiority. I concluded that God was mistaken to call me. Eventually, I realized writing wasn't a choice, but an obligation. The solution turned from quitting to learning that I needed education to perfect my skills. Just because we wish to quit doesn't indicate we're stuck. Even if it's impossible to change our dilemma, we can experience change while in it. Learn to press forward, reach out, allow others to touch us, and cry. Until we attempt the project, we'll never know how far we'll go.

If we inspect closely, we'll discover that right around the corner of an obstacle is a miracle much, much larger than the obstacle.

Press Forward

When we're pressing forward, we're going against the stream. This requires great effort and determination. By pressing forward, we're also leaving a walk of feelings to enter a walk of faith. Our position changes from feelings to trusting God.

I believe God wants me to succeed. I embrace this knowledge by trusting his word. If I endeavor to learn to control my tongue, I locate the necessary Scriptures, print them, and place them in areas of my house where I see them every day. I meditate upon their meaning and pray to implement changes where needed. In this same respect, if I desire to change a negative impression of God, I locate a specific truth about him in the Bible.

I cannot reject God when he tells me to lay aside every weight and run with endurance the race marked out for me (Hebrews 12:1). I must not ignore the encouragement that says, "Blessed is the man who perseveres under trial, because when he has stood the test, he will receive the crown of life that God has promised to those who love him" (James 1:12). I can apply Peter's instruction to my stress, "Cast all your anxiety on him because he cares for you" (1 Peter 5:7). Jesus tells me: "Therefore do not worry about tomorrow, for tomorrow will worry about itself. Each day has enough trouble of its own" (Matthew 6:34).

When these scriptures take root in my spirit, I rest assured in the knowledge worry is counterproductive because God is bringing to pass wonderful plans for success. I resist anxiety because I realize someone bigger is taking care of me. This prevents me from quitting because I've surrendered control to God. Daily, I practice making right choices.

The right choice begins with raising my head from the pillow, lifting my body to a sitting position, and swinging my feet to the side of the bed and on to the floor. I arise from the bed, enter the bathroom, and wash my face. I continue with prayer to God to enlist his assistance. I don't have to feel like praying. I don't have to feel anything. I do it because it's the right thing.

Irrespective of my feelings, I pray because I enjoy daily communion with God. To maintain excitement in my relationship, I employ change. Just as change invigorates a marriage, so it does with God. Sometimes I awaken wanting to return to bed. It's here I enter a creative praying mode by ignoring routine.

I may walk while praying, or change the position or room in which I pray. When words fail me, I turn to the Psalms and use the words of David to pray. Frequently, I write prayers in a journal. While writing, negative emotions surface that were previously hidden. Once these emotions appear, I can deal with them. Occasionally, I walk outside to pray or relocate to the park. Driving back roads uncovers nice places to pray. The presence of running water—a fountain or beach—is also helpful. Generally, a change of scenery helps me connect with God.

A vital aspect of prayer is silence. Sometimes, I push the mute button on all the noise. How do I listen to God if my world is noisy? How can he speak if I'm holding up both ends of the conversation? During times of silence, God reveals thoughts that contribute new insight into my situation. I may discover a need to forgive someone or a need for forgiveness myself. God may indicate areas of ministry in which I need to be involved, areas that bring great joy. I can't overemphasize the necessity of allowing God to be in charge.

Regardless of my feelings, I'm committed to daily Bible reading, journaling, and church attendance. Oftentimes, at my lowest point, God has supplied surprises at church.

One morning I was deeply depressed when I arrived to teach the young married class. I was recently widowed and felt hopeless. Despite the emptiness, I was prepared to teach. Not long after I entered the room, Rosa Lee, a woman of prayer, poked her head around the corner. She said, "God woke me at two o'clock this morning and laid you on my heart. I want you to know I prayed for you."

Immediately, my spirit lifted. *I'm not alone! Somebody knows where I am and cares enough to pray for me while everyone else is sleeping.* More than this, God knew my grief and enlisted the help of someone else.

Another part of pressing forward is learning about your situation. Educate yourself by reading, taking classes, making an appointment with a professional counselor, and joining support groups—becoming involved with people who identify with you. The more you understand, the better you cope. Don't live in defeat. Solutions exist.

Reach Out

Healing comes as I consider others in the midst of my personal crisis. When I reach out, God returns the favor. Reaching out prevents me from centering my attention solely on my needs. When others hurt, I hurt.

You're not denying your pain when you reach out to others during times of personal trauma. It's helping you to look temporarily beyond yourself. Healing is a lengthy process. You're not helped when you're constantly consumed with negative emotions. Ruth Senter says people have become so consumed with their own needs that they have become their rights.

> Some of us are old enough to remember LPRs (long playing records). One liability of LPRs was the dust that collected in the grooves and caused the needles to stick. Then you would hear the same note over and over and over until someone pushed the needle ahead.
>
> Maybe we are like a needle stuck in the groove of an old record album. Maybe we are stuck on ourselves. Maybe we are not moving on to the next note. Not getting over ourselves.
>
> Maybe we are so stuck on our needs that we are no longer sensitive to the needs of people beyond our own little inner circle of family and friends.
>
> Maybe we are so stuck on our needs that everything we do has this bottom line: Are my needs being met?

The trouble with needs is they keep expanding. Like a rubber band, you can stretch them out for a long, long way.[4]

Begin reaching out by praying for others in the same situation. When you feel lonely, pray for the lonely. When depressed, anxious, or fearful, do the same. This isn't overlooking your needs. This is offering space to heal. When you take care of the needs of others, God will take care of your needs.

You reach out by volunteering at the hospital, Red Cross, or at a home for unwed mothers. You offer to be a Big Sister. You visit a shut-in with warm conversation and a warm dessert. You surprise the pastor by offering assistance in the nursery.

Allow Others

In times past, I developed friendships, but I didn't feel I needed to be transparent. I believed God was all I needed. I didn't need people. I identified with Peter, who refused when Jesus asked to wash his feet. I washed others' feet, but allowing others to wash mine was difficult. Then I learned it wasn't necessary to carry the load alone. God had provided a caring community of believers to share the load. This turnaround came when a young Christian staff worker determined to enter my life.

My husband, Steve, battled lymphatic cancer intermittently for ten years. When it appeared the cancer would go into remission, another crisis occurred. We discovered he'd obtained hepatitis C from a blood transfusion. Because he was strong and otherwise healthy, we were optimistic he'd win this battle too. But he didn't.

I walked down the long hospital corridor to the intensive care unit. The faces I saw around me said something had happened while I was gone. *No, it couldn't have.* At twenty-nine years of age, I had not considered this option. The doctor was going to discover the raging infection in Steve's body, and he'd get better.

As I entered the room, members of our family stood around Steve's bed crying. Tears came quickly, but I didn't know why I was crying. *He couldn't be dead. He's too young!* I stared at his face as I waited for his eyes to move. I touched his hand and squeezed his fingers, but still no response. He looked dead. *But he can't be.* Twenty minutes passed before the nurse entered the room.

"What funeral home would you like his body sent to? Will you please sign a form to release him?"

I didn't want to make this decision without him. *This can't be happening.* In a fog, I gave her the necessary information and turned to unwrap the tape that held his watch to the bed rail. I mechanically slid it onto my arm. From the wall I removed a scenic picture that contained his favorite verse: "But those who hope in the LORD will renew their strength (Isaiah 40:31)." I held it close to my chest and left the room, looking back once more. *How can I leave him?*

Upon leaving the hospital, I tried to absorb this unbelievable news. When I arrived home, I went to the backyard—our favorite place to spend time alone. A track was nearby; I walked it for miles that night. *What was I to do? We never talked about this happening. I'm alone. How will I tell Joe?*

After I had walked for more than an hour, Lori, a church staff member, came to where I was walking. She didn't speak. I knew she cared. She had befriended me for several years. She quickly picked up my pace, placed her hand around my elbow, and walked with me—never talking. With every step, my self-reliance melted into the concrete.

The door opened another fraction two days after the funeral when she brought to the house the most delicious dinner I'd ever had. Her recipe for Chicken Parmesan is still my favorite recipe. In the weeks that followed, she continued to seek me out, not with a lot of words, which wasn't characteristic of her nature. I came to realize I wasn't alone. It felt good to have a friend.

Her friendship opened up a need for more friends. I'm glad she walked with me. I learned that friendship doesn't solely concern my gifts, but also focuses upon the gifts given in return. Friendship endures the lengthy struggles—when everyone else is long gone. She never leaves, even when you're grieving for many months. She doesn't think you're selfish. Friendship cries with you.

Friendship rejoices with you over every minute accomplishment. She'll even throw a party when the situation warrants it. She thinks your half-pound weight loss is incredible. She thinks the class you're taking is interesting. She cares about your day.

She keeps a confidence. She is always on your side, even when she doesn't take your side. She's nobody's "yes" person. She prays for you, counsels you, encourages you, and allows you to return all the favors. Intimate relationships are vital to your survival. Robert Fisher puts much importance on these relationships.

Despite what New Agers or secular humanists may say, man cannot begin with himself or look solely to himself for fulfillment and satisfaction. Someone has said, "The smallest package I have ever seen is a man wrapped up in himself." We need only to go to a mental institution to see the ultimate tragic results of a person totally focused on self. Regardless of one's mental state, egocentrism is a disease that plagues us all.[5]

Cry

The Bible's pages are a winding road of tears. These trails weave through Abraham's tears for Sarah's death and Jacob's for Joseph's apparent one. The trail continues as Esau wept when united with his brother Jacob and Joseph when united with his eleven. We drive around the corner to discover Hannah crying for her barren condition, then Jonathan and David weeping at the depth of Saul's hatred. It doesn't get better as we witness Hezekiah's tears at news of his prophesied death (see Genesis 23:2; 33:4; 37:35; 42:24; 2 Kings 20:3; 2 Samuel 1:17).

As we travel further, we hear the loud lament of Israelites concerning the death of their babies killed by orders from Herod. We contemplate Jesus as he weeps over Jerusalem and at Lazarus's grave. The road grows bumpy as Mary washes Jesus' feet with her tears and Paul cries for the people to whom he ministers. And the tears do not end here. (see Matthew 2:16–18; Luke 7:38; 19:41; John 11:35; Philippians 3:19).

These tears were evoked for different reasons: death, sin, remorse, unfairness, and division. Much hasn't changed through the centuries, for we continue to weep for these same reasons. Sometimes it seems these tears are for naught. But Scripture tells us this isn't the case. David says in Psalms 56:8, "Record my lament; list my tears on your scroll—are they not in your record?" When he says "scroll," he is also saying, "Put my tears in your wineskin or in your bottle." In those times, tears were captured in small vials and treasured. God notices our grief.

When we view tears as an item to be treasured, we understand they aren't wasted on God when cried in earnest. Psalm 126:5, 6 tells us, "Those who sow in tears will reap with songs of joy. He who goes out weeping, carrying seed to sow, will return with songs of joy, carrying sheaves with him." From this passage we understand that weeping must not hinder our sowing. Even though we're in sorrow, we continue our labor. We never stop. We also see that sorrow is not the end of the matter, even though in times of grief this may seem to be the case. After sorrow comes unending joy. Tears wash the soul of impurities. In the brokenness of our spirit, we release complete control of the situation. We don't have the answers, but God does. And we leave him to work it out.

Give yourself permission to cry. Make an appointment to do this now. You'll never be sorry. Don't wait for someone else to take the initiative. You take the lead. Tears are healthy.

Stop Waiting

We must stop waiting for someone else to acknowledge the sacrifices we've made. We must stop waiting for the other person who mistreated us to fail. Oftentimes, we place our lives on hold because we're waiting for the other person to act. If we can't handle another person's rejection, we must internally investigate the reason. When the truth is uncovered, pray for healing.

We make our own choices. We can't control another person's actions. Likewise, we mustn't allow another person to control us. When another person determines our state of mind, he possesses our control panel. Take ownership of the control device. No one controlled Jesus, and it isn't healthy to allow another to control us. Stop waiting for all the pieces to fit before making a decision to be happy.

You encounter people at your job who dislike you—stop trying to force their affection. Love them anyway. You inherit family members who reject you. Stop elbowing for accept-ance. Bless them anyway. You work for an employer who refuses to offer appreciation. Honor him anyway. You can't force others to recognize your needs. As much as it hurts, whether anyone ever acknowledges your efforts, you must not quit. Remember, no one can steal God's approval from your heart.

God places you in odd situations. Let's face it; this is a walk of faith. God sent Jeremiah forth to prophesy for forty years to people who refused to listen. How would you feel if God told you that you were wasting your breath, but to con-tinue preaching anyway? At least Jonah spoke to a group of people who listened.

The person you're pouting about may not realize his immaturity for another twenty years. You can lose a lot of liv-ing if you're waiting for him to apologize. You can chance it and devise a confrontation, but this isn't always the answer. You don't beat truth into people and neither does God. Stop waiting and leave him to God.

Some of you have endured the burden of expectations that didn't materialize. You dreamed of the perfect husband, but discovered flaws. You envisioned children who would follow the path you led them to, but they chose the rocky road. You saw professional success, a big home, flawless church members, financial prosperity, and understanding friends. This didn't happen, and you're disappointed.

Don't you think it's now time to bury those expectations you can't change and put your energy into areas you can change? Grieve, but don't stay here. You can build again upon these tears. You can build a healthy thought process. You can build a new trust in God. You can begin today. Do it.

I Can Do Something About This

I can do everything through him who gives me strength
(Philippians 4:3)

Pray
Dearest Lord,
I've wanted to quit _____. I have
not known what to do with my interruption of disappointment.
I know with your help, I can tunnel my way out of this. There are
other solutions and I must find them. Speak to me, even as you
heal me of despair and offer fresh hope. I am asking you in
the following exercise to bring to my mind every negative
thought I meditate on for more than one minute.

Find
Locate a glass jar and plastic bags that seal.

Purchase
Buy a bag of popcorn seeds.

Project
If you are away from home during the day, take
along two plastic bags. Write "seeds" on one and
"thoughts" on the other. In the seeds bag,
place a large handful of popcorn seeds.

Daily
Every time you meditate on destructive thoughts for
more than one minute without a solution, place
a seed in the thoughts bag. At the end of your day,
place all thought seeds in the glass jar.

Look

At the end of one week, look at the seeds in the jar.
Are you now more aware of these thoughts?

Make

Allow this to be a lifetime practice.

CHANGED
PERCEPTIONS
Overwhelming
Interruptions

THE CROSS OF SNOW

In the long, sleepless watches of the night
A gentle face—the face of one long dead—
Looks at me from the wall, where round its head
The night-lamp cast a halo of pale light.
Here in this room she died; and soul more white
Never through martyrdom of fire was led
To its repose; nor can in books be read
The legend of life more benedight.
There is a mountain in the distant West
That, sun-defying, in its deep ravines
Displays a cross of snow upon its side.
Such is the cross I wear upon my breast
These eighteen years, through all the changing scenes
And seasons, changeless since the day she died.

—HENRY WADSWORTH LONGFELLOW

Chapter
FIVE

The Clock
Strikes Death
Death's Interruptions

J UST AS I sat down to breakfast with family at a favorite
restaurant, the cell phone rang. With fork in hand I
glanced down at my plate covered in an array of southern
style favorites—bacon, home-fried potatoes, buttermilk biscuits, and sliced cantaloupe—but I hesitated to take a bite. As
I listened to the voice, I knew something was wrong. Bert had
died. How could that be? He taught Sunday school in our
church. He wasn't even thirty years of age. I lost my appetite.

Death does that—causes us to lose our hunger pains. It
interrupts our plans for a new colonial-style home with
granite countertops, double oven, abundant white cabinets

in the kitchen, and large custom-draped windows framing the view of our beautifully landscaped floral garden. The plan now burned at the stake, driven through the meat grinder, trampled in a rodeo stampede. Death forced the co-owner out of town.

Bert, a man in his twenties and in good health, dead of unknown causes. Calvin Miller says:

> Death is not a monster created by a power-mad theological Frankenstein to scare unthinking individuals around to their viewpoint. Death is a fact! It is a fact more unpleasant than life, but a fact as certain as life; it has a way of catapulting itself into all our unsuspecting moments. It becomes the grim reminder at every New Year's Eve party that we are not merely watching a clock; we are watching our passing.[2]

Death interrupts our fun. We laugh, but then suddenly realize something terrible happened. A sick feeling forms in the pit of the stomach. We laugh, and then check ourselves as if some strange noise emitted from our throat. How long had it been? We laugh, but its hollowness echoes back at us. We laugh, because we're tired of crying.

Death interrupts our job promotion. Our boss dies, and his brother, who seems to dislikes us, takes over the business. Employed by the company for forty years and less than ten years from retirement, our future is suddenly similar to the horror movies we channel-surfed past. For the first time, we understand death's interruption creates a trickle-down effect.

John F. Kennedy died and the world grieved, as if each one had personally shared dinner conversation with him the previous night. Princess Diana died, and so did our hope in a royalty we can touch. On September 11, four airplanes crashed into the Twin Towers, the Pentagon, the ground, and our hearts. Whether we knew one or two of the deceased or none at all, the horror of that moment emblazoned a reality of death we will never rub away with a pencil eraser or a washcloth or a gallon bucket of detergent. Death devastates, annihilates, humiliates, frustrates, and castigates. Death—the great interrupter.

Death interrupts our accomplishments. The thrill of success isn't nearly as powerful and satisfying without our loved ones applauding. Death interrupts our purpose. We begin to reevaluate our goals. We discard some and we gather a few others. Its knocking causes us to question things we ordinarily accept. Death brings out the best and the worst in us.

Death awakens within us a need to fill a void we are not aware exists. It's as if until this moment we've been asleep, or perhaps living on an isolated island, enjoying a separate existence without the reality of chaos and confusion. We've been lost in loving our children, absorbed in financial endeavors, accumulating furniture, cars, jewelry, clothing, and enjoyment apparatuses. We've been planning summer vacations in our minds, balancing our checkbooks, and thinking about tomorrow, all within the confines of each seven day week. Then death shrouds the beauty, enjoyment, tranquility, and purpose of the temporary.

When death enters the room, every preconceived thought presents itself for examination. Our luscious landscapes, the important bank account, our plentiful possessions, and the surrounding safety net of family and friends—each violently forcing us to evaluate our purpose in life.

We Avoid Death

Most perplexing to me is our avoidance of death. The subject that most greatly affects our future plans, changes our presumptions, and depresses our emotions. Rehearse the most recent conversation at the office. Did you share feelings on death? Would anyone want to be so morbid? Aren't office breaks and lunchrooms designated for lighthearted conversation? Sadly, when we are prepared to discuss death, it's often too late.

Mark Buchanan points to heaven. He says being aware of death makes us more aware of life.

> It keeps our appetites healthy, our wonderment sharp. It winnows clutter from our life. From the perspective of death, we learn to order our lives differently. "Teach us to number our days aright," Moses once prayed, "that we may gain a heart of wisdom (Psalm 90:12)." *Teach us to pray. Teach us Your ways. Teach us to number our days.*[3] (Emphasis added.)

The most crucial aspect of our existence is death, yet we find it irrelevant. How do we live if we don't know how to die, don't plan to die, and refuse to believe we will die? If our life's focus is living, then any accomplishment is temporary. But if we intend to live to die, then our purpose discloses a magnified passion.

God's Word reveals numerous instances where passion increases with impending death. Consider Belshazzar in Daniel 5. A hand suddenly appears and spells out his demise in letters on a wall. His knees knock. Or imagine the horror of living in the belly of a bad-breathed whale, of being thrown into a fiery furnace, of being locked in a rat-infested prison, of being thrown in a damp dark cistern, or of being challenged to fight three hundred men? Heaven draws nearer when the suspicion of death beats louder.

The Bible tells of a sick man named Hezekiah (2 Kings 20). Hezekiah was told by the prophet Isaiah to set his house in order because he was going to die. As a result of this revelation, Hezekiah cried out to God. He didn't want to die. And neither do I.

I desperately want to be present to celebrate my son's university graduation. I've paid his tuition, books, housing, insurance, medical, clothing, and food expenses for over twenty-two years. I anticipate the honor of dancing down the aisle with his diploma clamped between my teeth. I deserve the privilege of witnessing his retrieval of a job paying more than Monopoly money. An even greater day awaits when I am afforded the grandstand view of seeing him send his child through college wearing a "without a care in the world" smile on his face. My son is such a mother's delight.

Hezekiah was a parent too. He wanted to live, so he reminded God of his past accomplishments. He evidently pleased God with his request, because God granted him another fifteen years. I am glad to serve a God who listens and understands my needs to see matters through to completion.

Yet, the facts remain. Even though Hezekiah was granted an extension on life, he eventually died and I will too. Mark Buchanan encourages readers to face reality.

> I'm dying. Sometimes I forget it. Don't misunderstand: I am not, at present, suffering from a terminal illness or a mortal wound. I have no virus breeding, thick and septic, in my bloodstream, no genetic disease swarming, swift and

capricious, in my flesh. I am not, to my knowledge, dying soon . . . But I am, as the apostle Paul puts it, "outwardly wasting away (see 2 Corinthians 4:16)." That's what I sometimes forget: my mortality, my frailty, my life's brevity. "I will be the exception," I think, the one who evades death at each turn, slips its every snare, snatches hold of Elijah's chariot or Enoch's robe and, whisked into the wild blue yonder, remains unscathed by the grim reaper's scythe. . . .[4]

Death isn't easy and we ordinarily tend to avoid the uncomfortable. We lost another friend also, Roz. Unlike Bert, Roz knew death was drawing near and made preparations for it. He seized death by the throat and declared it had no power over him. He told his family and friends good-bye and then left. Before he left, I went to say good-bye.

As I entered his room, I struggled not to cry. Good-byes have never been easy. I stared into his face and attempted to memorize every feature. I dreaded the day when I would not hear his kind words, feel his pat on my shoulder, nor see those beautiful white teeth smile in my direction. Even more, I loathed the thought of his wife, Joanne, walking into church without him. *Oh, Roz, do you know how much you will be missed? Do you know how dearly you are loved?* I needed to say something—everyone else had—but the words stuck in my throat.

Peggy Noonan, a former presidential speechwriter, said:

. . . the true horror of death for survivors is not that we cannot go on without the one who died, but that we can. The extra grief of that going on, the fact that the rug of life has been pulled from under you and yet the next morning the birds sing, the paper hits the door, the lady from Visa calls to say you're overdue . . . this is the horror of death, the crudity with which it changes almost nothing. When, like Auden, you want the world to stop, the police to wear black gloves, the planes to write your sadness in the sky.[5]

The sadness of death has arrived. Much sooner than you anticipate, you not only ride in the processional but you also sit in the limousine. Whether you're ready or not, you must decide upon the funeral home, cemetery, burial attire, flowers, minister, service, pallbearers. Then the inevitable. You stand in a room filled with caskets while nicely suited attendants ask, "Which color would you prefer—blue, black, pink, brown, tan, or gray?" You chose gray. He would look nice in gray.

Then the funeral and burial. You feel sad and grieve your loss, yet quickly leave the graveside, step into your vehicle, turn up the radio, and drown out the finality of death. You don't want to stay here; the prospect is too painful to consider. Yet, without an invitation death comes closer. The music refuses to rise above it.

The Snowflake

I was twenty-nine years old when my husband, Steve, died from cancer. Our son, Joe, was eight. Before this tragedy, the gulf separating heaven and earth was a mere turning of the corner. Suddenly, I learned, it is a massive division and it lasts forever. Previously sheltered in a protective cocoon, this explosion of truth forced a crater to suddenly fill itself with warehouses of silence, grief, fear, anger, confusion, rejection, and despair. Through anxious moments, I eventually came to understand what I hadn't considered before. The simple reality of life escaped me. People live and people die. Not one, but all. And what becomes "we" through vows said in a church eventually comes back to "me"—all alone again.

Dear Steve,

What is life without you? A long journey to the bank to remove your name from our checking account. Calling the insurance company to say you are deceased. Sleeping on the couch because the bed's too large. Removing your pictures from the wall and putting them back in the same hour. Answering the telephone at noontime, always with disappointment. Wearing your flannel shirt around the house. Refusing to remove your watch from my arm. Waiting for the distinctive sound of your van to back into the drive. Running, running, running. Embracing the dilemma of whether to hang your stocking at Christmas. Leaving your razor, toothbrush and towel just like they always were. Wondering how to order pizza. Hating your workshop in the evenings. Coasting when all I can think to do is quit.

Your widow,
Lisa

Six months before Steve's death, while he enjoyed a stint of fairly good health and worked full-time, I attended a weekly women's Bible study and prayer group. On one particular Tuesday morning, after a season of prayer, I left the women's group spiritually energized.

I said, "Lord, I'll go and do whatever you want me to. Lead me." And he did.

Several miles from the church, I felt strangely compelled to enter the parking lot of a large pharmacy. Upon finding a space to park, I looked around to see if there was someone in the lot I should talk to. I didn't feel drawn to anyone, so I stepped out of my car and walked into the building.

I walked up and down the aisles as I questioned my reason for being there. After traveling the length of the store several times, my attention was strangely drawn to a white snowflake Christmas ornament enclosed in plastic and hanging from a metal peg. It wasn't particularly beautiful, but the words that arose in my heart were: *I will never leave you nor forsake you.*

Cheerfully I picked up the ornament, went to the cash register, and purchased it. Although nothing like this had ever happened to me before, I knew this was the reason I came.

I went home, found a tiny nail, positioned it in our front mantle, and hung my snowflake ornament from it. *I will never leave you nor forsake you.*

In the weeks and months that followed, Steve became very ill. His muscles cramped throughout his entire body. Sleep evaded him for many days at a time. He retained enormous amounts of fluid, which indicated a malfunction in his kidneys. I watched the twinkle in his dark brown eyes fade, his sexy smile diminish, his vitality weaken, his will to live crumble. Yet, I never stopped believing he'd make it. Something would happen—like a miracle. But it didn't.

In May, I rode with my brother for four hours to meet family in our hometown to find a casket to bury him. My son and I, as if in a trance, did everything we were supposed to. But it didn't make sense. With the help of family, we picked out flowers, greeted visitors, decided on the service, and waited in between until the day we were to return to our home.

I packed the car with our usual luggage. Steve was replaced with plants, flowers, cards, and food.

As Joe and I journeyed onward, we passed places we'd shared with Steve along this trip many times—the treed lot with water running along the backside where we hoped to buy land. We dreamed of building a log cabin—built high enough that we could fish from our back porch. We talked of filling it with handcrafted furniture, quilts, and my ruffled curtains. No more.

Still, zombie-like, we replayed a song on the tape player continually.

Can you see the clock from where you stand? Can you see the time by the pointing of the hands?

Soon before dark, we entered our driveway. With Joe beside me, we slowly walked to the door. As we stepped into the family room, my eyes surveyed its contents. The picture Steve purchased in Bermuda hung proudly on the wall. His gift to me—a treasured Royal Doulton doll stood erect on her shelf. My eyes misted over as they darted quickly across the room at the framed family photos, his easy chair, the handmade lamp, the pool stick case, the snowflake. The snowflake! *I will never leave you nor forsake you.* God knew.

God knew the day I married Steve. God knew we'd never share a twenty-fifth wedding anniversary. God knew that that previous Christmas was our last, that vacation our last, that picture taken our last. God knew we'd never buy the property, never plant another garden, and never fish at our favorite spot again. God knew, while I acted all along as if he didn't.

The Final Appointment

Peter Marshall once shared in his sermon, "Rendezvous in Samarra," an old legend about a merchant in Baghdad who sent his servant to the market. While the servant was shopping in the crowd, a woman he referred to as Death pushed him. The servant asked the merchant for permission to borrow his horse so that he could go to Samarra to avoid her. The merchant gave his consent and the servant sped away.

Later the merchant went to the market to find this woman called Death. He went to her and asked her why she had frightened his servant. Death replied, "I was astonished to see him in Baghdad, for I have an appointment with him tonight in Samarra."[6]

The point is not if but when. We all have an appointment. It's what we do with our allotted time until we keep our appointment that matters.

I enjoy *The Christmas Carol* starring Scrooge because he is presented with another opportunity to change. Reality teaches us that when the doctor delivers our termination papers we aren't granted another lifetime to retrieve our lost perspectives. But we do possess the moment. All isn't lost, yet.

A few years ago I began a journal listing the books I read throughout the year. Our son, grandson, and niece are also avid readers, so I encouraged them to do the same. I regretted that all the books I read in the previous forty years were not recorded in my journal, but I rejoiced because my son, grandson, and niece would not share this regret.

When our life comes to an end, everything isn't lost. We have a circle of people left to influence. If we have one hour to live, we can write a letter. If we hold one more day, it's possible to pen several pages of a book. If we're breathing another week, we can write a chapter. If we're granted a year, we can write the entire book. Yet, if not a book, consider the great benefits the world could receive from a letter. John Wesley did.

William Wilberforce was a member of the British Parliament in the late 1700s. For twenty years in the House of Commons, he fought to abolish slave trade. William felt sure he was acting on God's behalf. During this difficult time, he drew strength from a letter his dear friend, John Wesley, founder of the Methodist church, sent on February 1791.

> Dear Sir:
> Unless the divine power has raised you up . . . I see not how you can go through your glorious enterprise, in opposing that execrable villainy, which is the scandal of religion, of England, and of human nature. Unless God has raised you up for this very thing you will be worn out by the opposition of men and devils. But "if God be for you, who can be against you?" Are all of them stronger than God? O "be not weary in well doing!" Go on in the name of God and in the power of his might, till even American slavery (the vilest that ever saw sun) shall vanish away before it . . . That he who has guided you from your youth up, may continue to strengthen you in this and all things, is the prayer of,
>
> Your affectionate servant,
> J. Wesley[7]

Four days later, John Wesley died at the age of eighty-eight. William Wilberforce spent twenty-six years of his life to abolish slavery and at key times throughout the years, he reread this note to encourage himself. Wilberforce lived until he heard the news that Parliament passed a bill to abolish slave trade. Several months following his death, slavery was outlawed in all of the British Empire. Thank God for the letter that helped Wilberforce to endure this long struggle to victory. We can all write a letter. But some can do more.

The vast majority of us have more than an hour, more than a day, more than a month, and much more than a year. We must cherish this blessing of more and build it into a library that fills every home in America.

If I live for today without thought for the future, consider the sunsets I never rise early to sit under, the garden of cucumbers and tomatoes and okra and lima beans I never plant, the harvest of fresh vegetables I never reap, the person to whom I never offer a slice of butter pecan cake, the friend with whom I never share my favorite shopping extravaganza, the warm and gentle arms that never hug me, the accomplishment of writing my first book I never bask in. My refusal to consider the end result leaves me to mourn for the joy I never experienced because I never sat, planted, harvested, fed, built, hugged, received, or basked.

I must live today as if I will surely die tomorrow. I'll remember to kiss you good-bye. I won't forget to tell you how much I care because I want you to lovingly remember me. I'll clean my clutter, pay the last bill, call my friends, and apologize to my boss. I want you to say nice things at my funeral. I'll refrain from believing people will graciously throw in a kind word.

Like the house payment, the overdue notice will arrive in the mail. Some of us are living on borrowed time. While I don't desire to die today, I am prepared for the inevitable. Since I live in Florida, I'm squeezing all the juice out of the orange. I'm writing my letters today. I'm using my influence today. I'm forgiving today.

Death is a commonly shared interruption. Death costs us all the clothes in our closet, all the change on the dresser, all the gas in our tank, all the children swimming in the pool, all the ridiculous inventions we ever concoct. Death thrusts an unwanted stop sign en route to the amusement park. Even though death is delivered without my invitation, I will respond. I send either my passion or my passivity.

What will be my legacy? Will I be filled with deep regrets? Have I given my best, or have I a best yet to give? The grave is thirsty and is filled with billions. At least one more will follow.

He fought a battle—and triumphed.
He ran a race—and won it.
He charted a course—and finished it.
He had a faith—and kept it.
He set a goal—and reached it.
He sought a prize—and obtained it.[8]

—CHARLES W. CONN

I Can Do Something About This

I can do everything through him who gives me strength
(Philippians 4:13)

Pray
Dearest Lord,
May my life count. I don't want to suddenly wake up to realize
my life is gone, but I accomplished little. Help me to fulfill the
purpose for which I am created. I need your assistance in complet-
ing the following requests. I'm listening. I need you.

Evaluate
If I were told I would die tomorrow,
what would I do differently today?
Make a list.

Goal
Take the first item on the list and make it a goal.
On a separate sheet of paper, write the goal.

Plan
List ways you can accomplish this goal.

Write
Compose a letter to someone you'd treat differently
if you knew tomorrow was the last day of your life.
Tell this person where you were wrong and commit
to change the area(s) that affect him or her.

Give
At the appropriate time, give this letter to him or her.

I quickly zipped my dress and fled down the hallway toward the sound of a musical production that demanded applause. My feet clothed in sparkling black patent leather shoes began to wiggle and jiggle to the beat in an awkward imitation of a tap dancer. I felt the sun as it gleamed through the windowpanes and entangled its glorious rays in my golden curls. As I flung my ruffled dress in a swirling motion, my childlike exuberance proclaimed Jesus as Lord.

But then suddenly I glanced downward to discover ugly black marks marred my mother's polished hardwood floors. I ran to locate a cloth and after I vigorously moved it across the surface, the marks disappeared. I turned to the carpeted area, waved my cloth in the air and resumed my dance in ballerina style with an occasional elephant leap.

—LISA Q. HERRIN

Chapter

SIX

Surrendering
Everything
God's Interruptions

May 22, 1990
I came face to face with an undefeatable force. My precious hus-
band is dead. I never knew deafening silence before. God refused
me. I cried for the safe return to my mother's womb. She always
accepted me in her house, at her table—even when I felt God did-
n't care much for me.

"Lisa, God is asking you to give him your Isaac." My
friend meant to surrender my husband, Steve, to the Lord.

I can do this, I thought. *I'll nicely place him before the Lord like*
in the story of Abraham, and God will return him. I surrendered to
the request and waited, but God never relinquished him. He

died. For five months I waited. I waited until I came to terms with God that my definition of surrender and his didn't intersect. My husband wasn't coming home from work ever again.

My library didn't contain books on grief. I wasn't yet thirty. These events didn't occur to the young and handsome. I wasn't prepared. Old people die. Bad guys die. Not those passionate enough to dream. We never owned our cabin on the lake. We never fished from our back porch. We never planted our vegetable garden. Our plans were gone forever. I held them to my chest for a while. But then one day I looked over at my eight-year-old son soundly sleeping and knew I must go on.

Some say if we have faith in God, it miraculously overrides disappointment. I searched every crevice, but it cleverly hid itself. The magic formula didn't appear. King David never found it either. Maybe Abraham did. Or then maybe he didn't have as much to say as David.

Abraham had a son named Isaac. He was the son God promised to Abraham and Sarah in their old age. God told Abraham to take the son he loved and offer him as a burnt offering.

A burnt offering? The closest to a burnt offering I've witnessed is a pig with an apple in its mouth roasting over a pit. It wasn't very appetizing. I refuse to consider the possibility of my grown son rotating on a long metal skewer. I can't imagine the thoughts running through Abraham's mind. Perhaps he didn't think as I do, which made him God's man of the hour.

God interrupted Abraham in the form of a test. God didn't need to test Abraham for his sake, but rather for Abraham's sake. God knew the result before the test was given, but Abraham didn't. Tests reveal how much we've learned. Until we answer the necessary questions, we never know if we studied the books properly or listened to our instructor. Unless a test is administered we'll always wonder. Sometimes we're overly ambitious and falsely believe we'll receive a passing mark. Once the evidence is placed before us, we're sorely disappointed.

Tests uncover sin and character flaws. Evil lurks around the human heart seeking to devour it. How can we annihilate sins we're unaware of? Every destructive instrument crouching in the miniscule cracks of our mind must be named. What did Abraham's test present?

Upon close inspection of this particular test we realize Abraham learned a great deal. How did he become so wise? This wasn't his first test. Abraham encountered many tests, and he didn't pass them all. His life history displayed a series of accomplishments and failures.

Abraham was tested when he was asked to leave home to enter unfamiliar territory.

> By faith Abraham, when called to go to a place he would later receive as his inheritance, obeyed and went, even though he did not know where he was going. By faith he made his home in the promised land like a stranger in a foreign country; he lived in tents, as did Isaac and Jacob, who were heirs with him of the same promise. For he was looking forward to the city with foundations, whose architect and builder is God (Hebrews 11:8–10).

Tested

Abraham's first test was leaving home.

I grew up in a family with three siblings, a mother and a father. I was the only one who moved away.

Recently, I went home for ten days—a pleasant treat. I enjoyed the company of my family around the dinner table with the snow outside that kept us inside—warm, close to the fireplace, and to each other. Who in the entire world will ever love me like these people? They don't expect magnificent exploits of me. Even if I were to attempt greatness, I would remain the same in their eyes. Just Lisa. And I wouldn't desire anything more of them.

While I always enjoyed adventure, I also loved home. Large long-distance phone bills were a staple in the first year of marriage to Steve. I missed my parents.

My mom always applauded my successes and, like a child, I wanted to hear her praise for the completion of my first set of drapes, my first Sunday school lesson, my first article for the church magazine. I needed my dad to remind me how to wallpaper, to sew, to type. I wanted my parents to know my new friends, see my new home, visit my new church, and share my new husband. I wanted them to be a part of my life. In many ways, they were. But Abraham's family wasn't. He completely left home, never to return again. That was God's will.

When Abraham entered Egypt, God tested him again. Would he trust God to protect him and his wife, Sarah? Afraid for his life, Abraham decided to say Sarah was his sister when in fact she was his half-sister. The world says this isn't a lie, but instead truth in part. They would declare Abraham was justified in omitting the rest of the story, the section where he married his half-sister. Some argue we should negate the truth in matters of life or death. Others debate we can lie to avoid hurt feelings. Is it ever appropriate to deceive?

Abraham is tested when told he'd have a son.

Against all hope, Abraham in hope believed and so became the father of many nations, just as it had been said to him,

"So shall your offspring be." Without weakening in his faith, he faced the fact that his body was as good as dead—since he was about a hundred years old—and that Sarah's womb was also dead. Yet he did not waver through unbelief regarding the promise of God, but was strengthened in his faith and gave glory to God, being fully persuaded that God had power to do what he had promised. This is why it was credited to him as righteousness (Romans 4:18-22).

Even though my only son turns twenty-four this year, it's still possible for me to bear more children. At my age, I don't want more children. If I lived during Abraham's time I'd warn him to reconsider and talk to God again.

I'd say, "Abraham, this whole matter doesn't solely concern conceiving, the pregnancy, the diapers, the bottles, and the two a.m. feedings. Imagine how old you'll be when he's a teenager. You'll lose all your donkeys, your cattle, and your servants. You'll be broke!" Abraham wouldn't listen to me anyway. He's already persuaded.

With God's promise to Abraham came an extension of God's desire to share his dream with him. It's as if God is saying, "Abraham, I have big plans for you. I have people for you to meet, places for you to go. Before you awaits a whole world. As a result of my blessings, you'll never be the same."

With my second marriage came two adorable, three-year-old granddaughters who are convinced I can't wash my face, cook dinner, clean house, or fold clothes without their assistance. They want to be a part of my activities. It feels good to watch their tiny hands work. Doing it together is fun.

Just as my granddaughters need to join me, I need to partner with God—to share a dream with him. I believe he's saying, *Lisa, you can't imagine the places I plan for you to see, nor the people you'll meet, nor the opportunities yet to unfold. Lisa, you just wait.*

Sometimes waiting is difficult. God seems a little snail-like. My husband says, "Lisa, if you will slow down I will catch up to you!" (Yes, I have long legs.) We despise waiting.

Joseph waited thirteen years in slavery and imprisonment for God's deliverance. David waited fourteen years in exile before he became king. Israel had to wait for their Messiah and some are still waiting.

God seemed slow to Abraham and Sarah too. They didn't have a lot of years. They tried to speed up the process. They were behind a car crawling in the passing lane and longed to give it a little push. Just a slight shove sufficed. But it didn't work. They figuratively bumped the other car and created a mess. Using Sarah's servant to expedite God's plan wasn't a good idea.

Like all good stories, the significance lies not in the beginning or middle but in the finale. Abraham's promise is fulfilled. Abraham has a strapping young son and his faith is soaring. God delivered on His promise.

Through the various mountain and valley experiences, Abraham's character flaws are slowly exposed. Abraham is gaining strength for the next encounter with God. With every passing and failing mark, he is growing stronger—more trusting, more satisfied, more confident, more dependable, more adept, more like God. Abraham is ready for the test—the greatest interruption of his life.

God tells Abraham to take his only son, his miracle son, his beloved son, and take him to the land of Moriah to offer him as a burnt offering. Where was Sarah, the old woman who brushed against the gate of death to birth this child, while these plans were being made? We don't know. We suspect she wasn't around or Abraham wouldn't have left the house. But, maybe Sarah is older and wiser than me and gives her full consent.

Did Abraham allow God's interruption? Yes. By this time Abraham is conditioned to follow instructions. Does God come through? Yes. He provides an acceptable sacrifice. With Abraham's act of obedience we forget his previous sins. We rejoice as if his success personally benefits us. Ultimately it does.

God never tested Abraham in this manner solely for Abraham's sake. God tested Abraham as an example for the many generations who followed. It's as if God said, "I want to show you faith in action." Don't tell me how to live. Show me. Just like Abraham.

God models an objective by way of personal illustrations. This isn't unusual for God. When he desired to prove a point to Satan, he used Job to demonstrate. We're finite while God is infinite. Every act he commits has an eternal perspective. Here Abraham demonstrates faith at its best. This pattern we all must grasp.

Abraham passed the test. Abraham embraced the interruption. He heard the call of God. He surrendered Isaac. What is an Isaac to you, to me?

A priceless commodity?
A fantastic job?
A cherished wife?
A long-awaited new home?
A closet filled with designer clothing?
 An enviable golf game?
A sports channel?
A speedy computer?

A cruise on the Caribbean?
A trip to the lake?
Steve?

Surrender the Doughnut

Long before my plane departed for Virginia to visit my parents, I could smell the aroma of my favorite pastry made at Hall's Bakery. During the flight my mouth salivated over the rich fluffy white filling that (I'm convinced) can't be purchased anywhere else in the world. I'll eat at least three doughnuts during my stay. If they stay fresh, some will be neatly packed in my suitcase for my return flight. But what if God said, "No doughnuts this time, Lisa. I want you to give them up for me."

I've come to understand that God doesn't require great sacrifices of me without first beckoning me to bow to the small things first—such as giving up the doughnut.

God still interrupts me today. He's not asking me for the freezer burned food that nobody wants; he's asking me to give up my doughnuts. He wants that one thing we love—the house you've always dreamed of, the job you've worked many years to achieve, the adored husband of your youth, the promised   child.

When God interrupts us with his request, our misunderstanding hinders us. We believe God is removing something necessary for survival. We agonize with our beliefs saying we *must* have our spouse, our children, our house, our success, our health, our doughnut.

We forget that this great nation was birthed through the pain of loss. Martha Washington outlived two husbands and all four of her children. Jane Pierce, wife of President Franklin Pierce, birthed three sons, all of whom died before the age of twelve. Ida McKinley, wife of President William McKinley, birthed two daughters, both of whom died by the age of four. Margaret Taylor, wife of President Zachary Taylor, birthed six children, but only four lived to adulthood. Louisa Adams, wife of President John Quincy Adams, was pregnant eleven times but only three of her children reached adulthood. Death presents itself to the elite, the young, and the lovely. Who are we to believe we'll escape?

Because I serve God, does it mean he'll never remove something cherished from me, never lead me to a place I don't want to go, never allow me to be martyred, never break my heart? Why should I imagine myself exempt?

Why Surrender?

If I can give up a favored doughnut, I can surrender the whole closet crammed with my best dresses. Then eventually I'll deliver up my Isaac—what is *most* dear to me.

When God interrupted me with his request for Steve's life, I was confused. To explain, allow me to digress into the world of Hannah (1 Samuel 1–2).

Hannah grieved because she couldn't bear children. She went to the temple and presented her request to God. She asked God to give her a son and promised she would return him to God, if he would meet her request. Hannah conceived and bore her son and followed through with her promise.

Hannah's story isn't rational. Why return Samuel to the Lord? Samuel needs his mother and his father. Didn't God ordain the family unit? What happens when Samuel is afraid in the night and cries for his mother? It could scar him for life when Hannah walks away and leaves him with a stranger. Can't Hannah dedicate Samuel to God just as easily from home and wait until he is older to bring him to the temple? She deserves to keep this child awhile. She endured grief from the taunts of Peninnah, her husband's other wife, the wife who bore him children without giving them up.

Hannah is pushed at a moment of desperation to make a hasty promise. God will forgive her. Hannah brought Samuel to Eli, a man a bit askew in his thinking. He once accused her, a grief-stricken woman, of being intoxicated. How could a priest do such a thing? Even at this, Eli was a man. What did a man know about raising a child? Could a temple be a home to her son?

In my case, I struggled to understand why God took my husband when we had an eight-year-old son to raise. It wasn't rational for God to go against the family. We were young and had many plans for our future. Surely God wasn't against our plans. What about the "prophetic words" spoken over us? I couldn't ignore the scriptures pertaining to healing. Certainly I must believe that God would heal Steve. If I didn't stand on this promise, who would? But sometimes God acts out of character, or rather my view of his character. I am reminded to trust even when I don't understand.

Where Is God?

God interrupts us as we happily pedal along on our bicycle. He shoves a stick in the spoke of our wheel and suddenly we are at a standstill or fall on our face. Do we passively sit and happily sing a tune as a world of others race past us? No! We demand that the stick be removed. We don't like his interruption. When God refuses to remove the stick, we demand a little louder. We believe God is ignoring our rights. All day we sit, helpless in the ditch, waiting for God, but he is silent. Another day and yet another and another and another passes. We helplessly watch the merriment of others laughing as they roll along with a casual wave in our direction. God might be silent, but we aren't.

"God, don't you know it's dark? It's frightening to be here in pitch blackness. It's getting cold. You should be the God who blesses me. You're not doing your job. I thought I was the King's child. This doesn't feel much like royalty."

As wounded animals, we howl at God concerning his extension of loneliness. We think of nothing better than to have the stick removed so we may roll again. We ignore the hand extending the flashlight, the fur coat and gloves, the blanket and pillow, the cup and saucer. We refuse the provision because we can't accept that God has temporarily removed us from the race.

When we happily pedal along, no problems or interruptions, we never scream, "God where are you? I don't understand you!" We accept the course of each day. But when God pokes a stick in our wheel, we are forced to explore his nature. We are forced to discover who he is. We are forced to sit and search for God.

God's interruptions are not fun, but they do change our lives and compel us to raise our arms toward heaven and sing "I Surrender All."

I Can Do Something About This

I can do everything through him who gives me strength
(Philippians 4:13)

Pray
Dearest Lord,
I want you to be Lord of my life. Please show me any areas that I
have placed ahead of you. I believe your grace is sufficient to make
possible everything I surrender. I realize I cannot be complete
without surrendering everything. May your perfect will be done.

Wait
Listen for God. Know he will answer, maybe through
Scripture, a friend, preacher, or book.

Write
Write whatever God says on a slip of paper.

Purchase
Place this slip of paper into a helium balloon.

Pray
While holding the balloon in your hand,
share all of your feelings with God. Don't hold back.

Dearest Lord,
It all belongs to you—my time, my family, my possessions,
my career, my ministry. I give you every worry. I give
you every heartache. I give you every doubt. Take it
and transform it into peace, joy, love, mercy, faith.

Release

When you have said all you need to say,
release the balloon into the air.

Praise

Offer praise to God and receive his joy.

Courage and patience, these I ask,
Dear Lord, in this my latest strait;
For hard I find my ten years' task,
Learning to suffer and to wait.

Life seems so rich and grand a thing,
So full of work for heart and brain,
It is a cross that I can bring
No help, no offering, but pain.

The hard-earned harvest of these years
I long to generously share;
The lessons learned with bitter tears
To teach again with tender care;

To smooth the rough and thorny way
Where other feet begin to tread;
To feed some hungry soul each day
With sympathy's sustaining bread . . .

. . . But if I may not, I will only ask
Courage and patience for my fate,
And learn, dear Lord, thy latest task,—
To suffer patiently and wait.

—LOUISA MAY ALCOTT

Chapter
SEVEN

A Bandage
Doesn't Do
Suffering Interruptions

A T A WOMAN'S conference, more than ten years after Steve's death, the morning speaker focused her message on physical healing. Her words were extreme and shamed those who suffered from illness. My heart grieved as I remembered the years we believed God would heal Steve. I was convinced to the point that I failed to prepare myself for the possibility of Steve dying. Now those denied prayers rose to the surface.

The next day she spoke again, and my sadness turned to anger. Throughout the day my anger grew to burning rage. A group of singers began to sing about the healing of God and various women came forward to testify of God's healing power in their lives. I stayed seated, but my emotions screamed at God.

"God, what kind of testimony do I have? You heal others and I'm left with death. I feel rejected. You denied my request and with your hand ground me to powder."

In an instant he spoke words, which healed my long-ignored wound. *Lisa, yes, it was as if my hand came down and ground you to powder. But do you know I've been collecting the powder all these years and using it to conform you to my image? Now you tell me, what is the greater miracle?*

I was mistaken in my belief that God left me to suffer alone with life's horrible twist. Suffering has a way of deceiving us into believing we've lost our lifelines. Our only thought is the pain and a quick escape from it. We fail to retain the thought that good will come from it. During these difficult periods, it's important that we have an arsenal of faith stored in our warehouse.

Broken Pieces

I remember when I first became aware of God's work to heal my brokenness. After Steve's death, I refused to sleep in my bed. And Joe hated his bed. Even a year after Steve's death, I continued to sleep on the couch and Joe made my bed his nightly abode. One evening I awakened to a loud crashing noise. Convinced that someone had broken into our house, I carefully searched each room with a flashlight. Although fear once would have been my first reaction, this was no longer the case. After Steve died, I was never afraid to be alone in the house. It was as if God provided an extra angel to protect Joe and me.

After searching the rooms, I returned to the couch to discover a shelf had broken loose from the wall. The items that had been on the shelf appeared to be broken. I was glad it was nothing more. I left it until morning.

The next day as I gathered the debris, I noticed that one of the items was a vase we had received as a wedding present. As I collected the tiny broken pieces and held them in my hand, a sad truth became clear. This vase in all its elegance was like my marriage—gone forever. It would never be repaired. It would never adorn my shelf again. I must gather the pieces and discard them.

Then I looked in horror at the exquisitely designed, porcelain Royal Doulton doll I had received from my Aunt Stella. The beautiful Blithe Morning who once graced the shelf with her hand to her hair, her multicolored red scarf draped around her shoulders with her hat in the other hand, now lay in ruins. Staring at the mess, I wondered about her future.

Lisa, you are like Blithe Morning. You once fell from a shelf along with the vase. While the vase—the marriage—will never come together again, the doll can be repaired.

As I carefully studied the broken parts, I realized the doll wasn't utterly destroyed. She could be glued together. She wouldn't be the same, but she'd be okay. And I would too.

I surrendered to the sovereignty of God. Others may have it all figured out. They may have God's plan for my life written neatly on scrolls, bottled, and sent out to sea. But I don't.

My experience taught me that God doesn't treat us all alike. Some of us travel by way of the desert and others by mountain. Some go by the scenic route and others through cow pastures. Some plant gardens from which they never eat, build houses in which they never sleep, invest in stocks from which they never profit. Yet, all who obey God are blessed—just a little differently.

Oftentimes, I thought I knew better than God. I thought the highway far better than the byway and the familiar path superior to uncertain terrain. At times I've desired to tell God how to run the planet, but at other times I'm glad I don't hold the atomic bomb detonator.

Suffering As An Enemy

I don't stand outside on the front porch and wave to "suffering," inviting him to dinner. If suffering telephoned me, I'd tell him to mind his own business and not to call again. Furthermore, I'd tell suffering never to enter my yard. Suffering is useless in assisting with household repairs. I don't do well when the hammer hits my unsuspecting finger, when the screwdriver falls and lodges upright in my big toe, when I've drilled a hole in the wrong place, or when I've hung the wallpaper upside down. Suffering is as unwanted as rats in my attic, leaks in the roof, and stains on my white carpet.

I'd much rather breeze past the job termination papers on my desk. I'd prefer not sign them, but instead I'd like to send them sailing off to another desk—to somebody I don't know. I'd rather set a dinner table for five than microwave a frozen dinner for one. I'd rather take a dip in a Florida pool than dive through an Alaskan ice pond. I'd rather shop for a nightgown at Victoria's Secret than be fit for a prosthesis at the medical supply store. But nobody asks what we prefer. Sometimes we must eat what the cook dishes up—or starve.

Suffering doesn't ask permission to enter our home. Despite all attempts to divert him, he barges in unannounced.

Like an unwanted visitor he takes up residence and refuses to leave. We attempt to bodily remove him, but to no avail. We call for the police but they refuse to answer our call. We stand outraged, demanding our rights, but it seems nobody is listening.

Our insistence to rid ourselves of our enemy, suffering, is much like the main character in the movie, *The Terminator*. Arnold Schwarzenegger took his job as terminator seriously as he pulled out his high-powered weapons and blew the bad guys away. Although we don't want them dead, sometimes we'd like to force a few people out of town. Send them on a one-way trip to Africa.

We pull out every piece of ammunition in our arsenal. We seek the refuge of the Lord and attempt to hide, but suffering hunts us down. We pull out the sword of the Spirit and we rip him to shreds, but he will not die. We call in our friends to stand watch, but he slips through the cracks unnoticed. We turn up the sound on our stereo but we cannot drown out his noise. We cry, we scream, we beg, but the misery will not leave. God seems to be on another planet visiting his other friends.

August 19, 1990
When I stop too long I always wander back to Steve. For the last few weeks the terrible realization set in. Steve is not on a business trip. He is not coming back ever again. The truth tormented my mind repeatedly. "He's not coming back. I must go on." Sometimes I don't want to go on. I want to die. I have waited these last three months for the rapture to remove me from this world. God has not. I am angry. I cannot force Steve's return and I cannot follow

him. I never knew I could cry these many tears, which change nothing. Oh, for grace to trust God more. I must come to an end of myself. I am pathetically emotion driven. The Spirit of God must lead me. Oh, that I could commune with my Lord and feel his presence again. I feel so lost in the midst of this great salvation.

But then one day the wind stops howling, the hail no longer demolishes our vegetation, the rain isn't beating on our roof and all is quiet. From our hiding place, just like Noah, we send out a dove to inspect. He comes back with an olive branch in his mouth. We slowly walk toward the windows and peer through the heavy drapes. The sun is shining and all has been restored as if the storm were nothing but a bad dream.

Meaning in the Suffering

Drs. Cloud and Townsend tell us that when we come to the realization that pain can work toward our benefit, we make progress.

> When we give up protesting about pain and problems, we begin letting go of things that we can't keep anyway. We learn what choices, paths, lessons, and opportunities are ours, and we enter the place of acceptance. We accept that pain is part of life. We accept that we don't have all the answers. We accept that problems will always be around us. We accept that there are some problems that will remain mysteries until we are face to face with God.[2]

We surrender our resistance when we accept that pain is inevitable. We continue to progress when we find meaning in the suffering. And finding meaning is sometimes similar to a search for a lost tooth on the beach. How do we make something good out of death, loneliness, financial ruin, defamation of character? How do we reach past the pain to receive anything meaningful?

Suffering causes us to turn inward. We can't reach around the excruciating pain from this third-degree burn on our chest. The pain invades our sleep, food, and work. We can't talk to others without discussing it. Suffering is the focus of all our attention. We attend to its daily care with antibiotics, cleansing, creams, and bandages. We medicate ourselves to bring temporary relief. Our first request is the removal of the pain.

Philip Yancey writes about Dr. Paul Brand, who thanked God for pain. Dr. Brand worked with leprous patients. Oftentimes, these patients lost limbs due to minor injuries. The absence of pain caused their burns and wounds to remain untreated, which resulted in serious infections.[3] Pain over the heart or down the left arm can indicate a heart malfunction. Pain in the side can mean a ruptured appendix. Pain in the eyes can represent a tumor. It's in the absence of pain that we fail to explore for causes.

Pain tells us the stove is hot and we must quickly remove our hand from it. Pain says to pull the tack from your foot before it drives deeper. Pain is like a car dashboard indicator light. Something isn't working correctly under the hood. Emotional pain is a signal that something happened that adversely affects us. It's when we're emotionally removed from feelings that we encounter a greater crisis.

Pain causes us to seek healing and solutions. We're not complacent when struck with suffering.

As we fumble with our suffering, we discover meaning when we realize we benefit from it. Even Jesus found meaning in his suffering. He understood why he had to suffer persecution and rejection. He understood why he had to be beaten and nailed to the cross. He understood the glorious end. We must do likewise.

Loneliness is transformed into meaning when we determine to use it to bring healing to others. Slander is transformed into meaning when we model for others Christ's example of forgiveness. Financial ruin is transformed into meaning when our trust in riches becomes a renewed trust in God. Death is transformed into meaning when heaven becomes nearer. We walk in meaning when we seek to learn through our crisis.

Suffering becomes our friend when we understand that nothing is wasted in God's economy. We continue in this friendship when we firmly accept the Scripture verse as truth which says, "weeping lasts for a night."

Some of the greatest physical pain is suffered through childbirth and kidney stones. We know that a woman suffering labor pains can endure the process because she believes the end result will be a beautiful baby. But for the person suffering from kidney stones, nothing good seems to result.

Emotional suffering contains the same dilemma as that of kidney stones. No purpose comes to mind when we're in the throes of agony. Nothing comes to mind but the suffering. Is it possible to find resolve while residing in the center of despair?

If kidney stones have a reason to sustain me to the end, I must find this reason. If loss of life has a reason that gives me hope, I must endure it. If a car accident has a reason pertinent to my survival, I must dig through the rubble to uncover it. In some cases, such reasons exist. A good detective will not relinquish her investigation until she discovers enough evidence to convict the guilty and be free. We may never know *all* the answers, just enough to keep our faith strong.

Branded

For many weeks I petitioned God on behalf of my brother, Ken, who was in a personal crisis that seemed endless. When it appeared utterly hopeless, God spoke to my heart—*I am branding him with my love.* I accepted the adversity in Ken's life as an act of God's will to conform Ken into His image. Through time as his troubles diminished, his love for others increased.

After these years, I slowly dissected the branding process, human suffering, and the love of God. I contemplated the compassion that flowed in various individuals, both contemporary and biblical. Eventually, a common thread emerged. These individuals suffered greatly. God's love came to them at great cost—by the fire of affliction. This branding process, although painful, leaves behind an indelible mark—love.

Branding cattle cannot occur without fire. Love cannot be birthed without fire. If you've encountered a compassionate person, understand he or she did not come to love without great personal pain—intense suffering and loss.

March 3, 1992
Dear Lord,
When Steve died I could not deal with the intense pain. I worked night and day, always running from the suffering.

Now I must work through the final obstacles. I hate the irritating sound of the phone and the clanking mailman's truck. They never bring good news. I wish my doorbell would never ring again. Regardless of my tears, nothing changes. I am locked in the spell of this stranger called grief. My life never changes. It is empty and miserable. I am tired of every day. I beg you to please help this poor pathetic human being. I have no control over my feelings. I am on a roller coaster edging to destruction. Yet, I feel I am nearing the close of this long and difficult trial. No one can bring happiness or peace but you, my Lord. Complete victory is lurking around the corner to capture me. I'm almost there.

What have I learned? I used to preach the word. Now I feel the word. I once tried to make others do right; now I understand why they do wrong. I saw the divorced, widowed, lonely, depressed, discouraged and prayed with them. Now I weep with them.

Now I understand the hurting, confused, and dying. They have been lied to, cast down, and sentenced to hell. They feel no way out. They see no hope. They find no solutions. They reach out for help and they find none for there is no life, no hope, and no answers outside of Jesus Christ. Yet, I must give my life for them for you gave your life for me. I must go on.

Carol Terry Talbot as a teenager at Woodbury College in Los Angeles felt money could buy everything she wanted, including happiness. But one day God convicted Carol of her materialistic dreams and she received his call to the orphans of India. On her way to India, war was declared on Japan for the bombing of Pearl Harbor. During a stop at Manila, the Japanese captured her along with others. She was a prisoner for more than three years.

While a prisoner, Ms. Talbot was stricken with impetigo. Sores covered her face to her feet. She contacted beriberi and nearly died from starvation, oftentimes scrounging around for weeds to eat. In 1945, she was freed. Of her experience in captivity she wrote:

> During the time spent recovering my health, lost through starvation and disease, God lifted my eyes to far horizons where I was to realize his reasons for my prison camp years, and the purpose for which I was on this earth.

After Ms. Talbot's recovery in America, she went on to India where she spent the next twenty years ministering, making it possible for thousands of people to have a Bible in their own language.[4]

Suffering Pays Well

Anything we receive from God comes with a price. For Abraham to receive the covenant, he had to leave home. For Noah to be spared, he had to build an ark. For Moses to part the water, he had to ride in the water. For David to be king, he had to save the king. For Lazarus to walk, he had to wait. For Jesus to give life, he had to die. For John to be a revelator, he had to be isolated.

Love doesn't just happen because we will it to. Knowledge doesn't come through holding our hands to heaven. We enter a process of growth. Education costs us—always. We must surrender to the process. Be willing to pay whatever costs are necessary. Then go forth as Elijah, all in his timing after we've completed the process. Spiritual maturity is important to success.

We live in a dangerous day where comfortable feels too good. We'd rather have free tickets to the game. Credit card accounts flow through our hands like water. We don't want to pay the necessary costs. We're hitching free rides. Some feel they are owed a world of favors even if someone else must work to feed them. But it's never free. If you are not paying your share, somebody is footing the bill. We must ask ourselves if we're spending our lives riding on the backs of somebody else's blessings.

There's nothing like owning your own success. To know you've worked a hard day and deserved your pay. To save for a car for which nobody else can call the note. To receive the title to the house you've paid on for thirty years. To receive the degree you've spent eight years obtaining. To bask in the anointing for which you've surrendered your life to God. Suffering amounts to the same thing. We know we didn't slide into leadership without its sting.

The Result—A Better Good

Some people take their grief to the rear window of their automobiles with decals expressing loving memories of deceased friends or family. Others advertise their loss in the newspaper with poems and brief messages. Still others place small white crosses next to the interstate. Then there are those who establish memorial funds, name buildings, and join causes to alleviate the pain of suffering. We can't idly stand by. We must do something with our pain.

Sometimes we don't have enough shoulders to cry on. We wear out one friend and then start on another. When she needs a break we continue with another until we're back to the first person. One friend can't bear the load of our suffering alone.

An important part of sharing our pain with others is teaching them to help us. Sometimes our friends don't know what to do. We can help them by explaining what we need, whether it's a hug or words that say they care or simply their presence without touching at all. When they attempt to correct you for making honest statements they feel aren't spiritual, teach them that you're offering truthful statements and that you don't require fixing. God isn't offended with your pain. You merely desire to be understood and comforted.

But then sometimes we don't know what we need and we don't have the energy to help others help us. During this time, smile and forgive often. Look into their hearts and know people genuinely want to help.

Suffering may seem like a mountain—we can't get around it and certainly not over it. The steps we take seem insufficient for the monumental task. Despair doesn't have a plan. God points us toward those who are suffering and says, "Look how many years they've suffered. It will be no different with you. You'll suffer until you die." At this point, we have a choice. We either ignore the Lord or we listen. We grow by asking God to show us how we can learn.

I heard a story of a man in his late fifties who was unjustly fired from a prominent position. Being near retirement, he had strong reasons to despair. But his Christian faith shone forth as he refused to be angry or bitter toward his supervisors. He determined that God knew the circumstance before it happened and allowed it to take place for a reason. He felt his life was in God's hands and that God desired to teach him something through this ordeal. He used his severance pay to refresh his spirit by vacationing. Soon after he returned, God answered his prayers by giving him reasons for his job loss. He had negative character traits that God desired to correct. By strengthening these flawed areas, he obtained a better job. Calvin Miller says, "Life is only painful when we cannot think why it was given to us. . . . We find that if we know the why of living, we can put up with any how."[5]

God is working a better *good* through the avenue of suffering. Oftentimes, we lose sight of this because of our unfamiliarity with suffering. We are like someone observing a hospital operating room scene for the first time, seeing the room filled with surgeons, nurses, and other medical specialists. One unfamiliar with hospitals might think these people were a band of criminals out of a horror film. He would see the staff using knives, tying the patient down, and preventing him from breathing by suffocating him with a clear plastic cup. He wouldn't understand that they were helping the patient.

The same is true of God and suffering. He is doing spiritual surgery. He uses devices and skills that are totally foreign to us. If we trust the skill of our master physician, we're spared much worry. We have no need for concern when we're on his table.

Although suffering seems to be a lonely place, you're assured through history and current news that many have suffered before you, many suffer around you, and many will follow you in suffering. Even though some of you scream a little more loudly than others, that doesn't negate that everyone will suffer. You just do it differently.

You have important decisions to make about suffering. You can choose to deny it. Prevent it. Cuddle it. Destroy it. Share it. Or learn from it. Hopefully, you'll learn from suffering and become a stronger Christian as a result. You'll be able to give to others in need of the same comfort you received. And you'll whittle out a mold others will desire to emulate.

I Can Do Something About This

I can do everything through him who gives me strength
(Philippians 4:13)

Pray
Dearest Lord,
I've had difficulty with suffering. I haven't known
how to handle it. Help me to find meaning in my
suffering and to become a stronger Christian as a result.
May you be glorified in my life as I take this
suffering and use it to comfort others.

Find
Look in your yard for a small stone.

Praise
Allow this small stone to be a memorial stone
praising God for the step you took today.

Place
Take your stone and place it somewhere
you can see it every day.

Find
The next day, look for another stone.

Discover
Allow this stone to be a memorial stone that represents you
being a step closer to discovering meaning in your suffering.

Place
Take this stone and set it beside the other.

Find
Locate yet another stone on the third day.

Reach
May this stone reach into the hope that
you will soon be able to help others.

CHANGED PERFORMANCES
Overcoming Interruptions

Do all the good you can,
By all the means you can,
In all the ways you can,
In all the places you can,
At all the times you can,
To all the people you can,
As long as ever you can.

—JOHN WESLEY[1]

Chapter
EIGHT

Headed for Hope
Purpose-Filled
Interruptions

I BECAME INVOLVED with a weight-loss support group. This helps me keep better tabs on my weight by making me accountable. An added bonus involves the sharing of great recipes. Recently, the leader asked the members if they exercised during the previous week. In a room of more than thirty women, no one had exercised—not even me. We left the meeting promising to do better the following week. We're busy and exercise is difficult to fit in—or so we say.

When it comes to exercise, we're in an addictive cycle. We realize we need to be more active, yet we purchase a riding lawnmower because it saves time. But when we feel guilty about our lack of exercise we take the time to jog three times a week. We say we don't have time to clean our house so we hire someone, then we again feel guilty about our lack of exercise and join an aerobics class to sweat for three hours every week. Then we don't have the energy to wash our vehicles, clean the pool, and mow the lawn, so we hire people again. We thrice feel guilty about not exercising and buy a treadmill. Exercise confounds us.

The same situation exists in the spiritual sense. We enjoy the meal—the sermon. We bask in the refreshing presence of God, but the activity part frustrates us. We're aware of the benefits of exercise—we feel better and we know that when we're busy helping others, we feel better. What prevents us from fulfilling another resolution to become more involved? What can nudge us into a lifetime commitment toward fulfilling our purpose?

Rejecting Our Purpose

When God reveals our purpose, he's pointing toward our future. When we reject our purpose, we look back as the Israelites did toward Egypt. To go back is to be willfully disobedient. This always results in sorrow. Fulfilling our purpose brings great joy into our future.

Why do we reject our purpose? Fear is one answer. The Israelites' fear aborted their purpose. They were expected to enter Canaan and conquer the land, but they saw themselves as small and the enemy as big. Furthermore, they saw God as small and the situation as large. As a result of refusing their purpose, they reaped destruction. They wandered in the wilderness until they died (Numbers 13, 14). God didn't consider fear a good excuse. God requires our trust.

The angels came to deliver Lot and his family from the destruction of Sodom and Gomorrah. They were given explicit instructions not to look back. But Lot's wife wasn't convinced of her purpose, so she looked back. Ultimately, the destruction destined for Sodom and Gomorrah also came to her (Genesis 19).

Consider the hypothetical sisters Candi and Mabel. Much like Cain, Candi rejects God's instructions and, like Abel, Mable is the recipient of a sibling's disobedience. Candi rejects God's invitation to minister to children. She wants the good life, filled with parties and fun. She shuns tradition, etiquette, education, moral standards, laws, religion. But she desires their benefits: respect, prestige, confidence, acceptance, maturity, and God's approval. Candi despises Mable because she possesses all strong attributes.

Candi isn't willing to pay the price of obedience, education, and hard labor. She scoffs at authority and shuns discipline. She's reaped illegitimate children, financial loss, and broken relationships. Candi isn't satisfied with her results. She has rejected her purpose and she can't stop looking over her shoulder.

Candi covets Mable's job, husband, reputation, home, friends, and children. Candi desires everything that belongs to Mable, everything except God.

Candi murders her sister's reputation because she's unwilling to make the required sacrifices. Jealousy consumes her as she falsely accuses Mable to her friends in private conversations. She can't look ahead because she's consumed with looking around. She can't look up because she fixes her eyes on a downward spiral.

Candi's rejection doesn't negate the fact God has a purpose

designed for her. Daily she is presented with opportunities to take a detour away from her destructive path. Her rejection of the truth curses her. The way of Cain is hard. The choice lies in what we accept. The blessing is always within our reach.

Hindrances to My Purpose

Even if we're not jealous of another, his or her success can intimidate us. Our inadequacies go a long way in hindering our purpose. We speak negative things to ourselves when we're in this frame of mind. We're plagued with thoughts such as, *They'll prefer my sister because she's more qualified for the job. She has respect in the community. She's more creative.*

I've discovered that God doesn't always call the smartest, prettiest, or the most efficient for the job. He doesn't always call the most spiritual one either. Occasionally, we wonder what in the world God is thinking when he calls some people. Maybe that's the way people felt when I was offered a job far above my qualifications.

A respected but temporary position became available in the women's department of my denomination. I soon became aware that I was going to be asked to fill the position. This wasn't what I prayed for. I asked God to place a certain woman in this position and to make me her gofer.

If I had presented an application for the job, I'd have been laughed out of the office. There were numerous others much more mature, spiritual, and knowledgeable. But I soon came to understand this was God's will and the revelation came through a dream. Why a dream? Some people require more and at this moment I needed a lot more.

I don't know the reasons God wanted me there, but I am fully aware it served his purpose in preparing me for future ministry. God doesn't always explain. This is why obedience is vitally important. If we ponder upon our inadequacies in every situation, we'd be rendered ineffective for every request for assistance.

God's measuring standards are an enigma. I look around to see the scales appear tipped in another's favor. Mirrors and scales are strange things; some mornings I wake up feeling heavy. I look in the mirror and say, "Yep, you're a real porker, girl." Although I'm not excited to jump on the scales, I peel down to bare essentials and step up. My weight's the same. Unbelievable! At other times, I wake up feeling like Twiggy, but against my better judgment I run to the scales to discover I've gained two pounds. It isn't fair.

While I battle pounds, other women are eating pound cake. While I pay Weight Watchers, they eat PayDays. While I eat nonfat everything, they eat hot dogs, fries, and chocolate shakes. They actually eat Twinkies to lose weight.

Then we have the other half. I meet women who wash their face in Ivory soap and use a Vaseline mask, and their skin is gorgeous. My face products cost more than my wardrobe.

I meet women who are articulate, while I have problems pronouncing words. I saw one deliver her passionate, perfect forty-minute speech without a single note. I can't remember the title without looking. I can memorize eight verses to quote and forget every word when I stand before a crowd.

I inherited lily-white skin, so I burned and freckled in the sixties and seventies when tan was in. How utterly uncool. While my friends enjoyed the lake, I invented excuses until I learned I could receive a tan directly from a bottle.

I arrived at the lake to meet my teenage friends, so happy with my tanned body. I held my head high and thought I was Miss America in person—until I walked into sunlight to discover rust around my knees, ankles, and elbows with hideous bright orange streaks crawling up my legs. Brown dirt beads rung around my neck. The only parts of my body unaffected were the unexposed places. My friends said I looked like I had a skin disease. The worst part was the revelation that it didn't rub off with soap and water. I was stuck with this "deformity" for what seemed like eternity.

Eventually I got over it. But singing is another matter. I enjoy making music while home alone. My husband teases me about my off-key tunes. I say, "Well, it's a joyful noise to God." He replies, "It's a noise, all right." Occasionally, at night when I'm being particularly playful, I say, "Baby, let me sing for you." His comical response is, "Maybe tomorrow." To which we both laugh.

Some of us work at everything while others wake up in the morning with sweet breath. I wonder if they use brand name Odor-Eaters in their shoes. Does their nail polish chip? Why doesn't their lipstick eat off? Surely their clothes automatically press themselves!

Okay, so details refuse to deposit in my memory bank. My tune and the composer's reside in different states. Yes, and a single doughnut packs a dozen to my hips. Mornings don't dance well with me and the black-and-white ivories stick beneath my fingers. Unfortunately, this sense of hopelessness pervades when I look over my shoulder. But the Holy Spirit refuses to allow me to continue along this path.

Yes, you're short-waisted, fair-skinned, and a little dingy, but I like disproportionate, pasty, wacko women. So what if your music is wasted at the symphony? I rather enjoy your flavorless tune. Your best will always fall short of somebody's in the room, but your sacrificial offerings make me glad.

One of the most humbling portions of my existence is the realization that God loves me despite the flaws.

Listen for My Purpose

Your purpose is a mystery. Even thoughts of it don't excite you. You're leery about conversations with God—too weird. You'd rather ignore this chapter and be happy for others. You'd prefer family fun until you reach heaven. Life's too complicated when too many people enter. Keep the numbers down. Be safe.

Have you consulted Jesus concerning this matter? Will he excuse ignorance forever? Jesus describes mediocrity as a position of lukewarm, and it doesn't settle well on his stomach. He'd rather you were hot chocolate or icy strawberry smoothie. He desires a fervent embrace, a firm handshake, a passionate gaze. I understand.

If you're my friend, be my friend. Stand by me when I need someone to hurt with me. Defend me when I'm slandered. Work with me to accomplish goals. Rejoice when I'm successful. I'll do the same for you.

If you're my enemy, show your rascally face. Don't deceive me with a friendly look while fraternizing with the devil. Let's clear the air and know where we stand. If you must, hate me to my face. I despise hypocrisy and so does Jesus. He desires devotion and loving submission as women in times past modeled.

God has always talked to women about their purpose. Jochebed, Moses' mother, accepted her role when she birthed her son, foresaw his ministry, and sought to protect him (Exodus 2). Sarah discerned her purpose in birthing Isaac and became the "mother of nations (Genesis 17)." To fulfill her purpose, Esther was willing to lose her life for the sake of her people (Esther). Anna the prophetess knew her purpose was to intercede (Luke 2:36, 37). Priscilla received her ministry alongside her husband (Acts 18:24–26).

Thecla of the first century church is the most famous missionary of her day. She held a dynamic ministry of preaching, teaching, healing, and baptism.

Paula (AD 347–404) was a wealthy Roman woman. When her husband died she used her fortune to build hospitals, monasteries, and churches, and the famous Church of the Nativity, thought to be located at the birthplace of Jesus. Paula's gifts were used to give the world its first popular Bible, the Latin Vulgate.

Queen Elizabeth of Hungary (1207–1231) used her vast wealth to care for the elderly and the sick, especially the lepers. After her husband died, she was banished from her home. At the insistence of the pope, she was restored to the palace only to eventually renounce her family, wealth, and pomp to perform works of charity among the elderly, the lepers, the poor, and the ill.

Catherine of Siena (1347–1380), although poor and uneducated, obeyed the voice of God and challenged the church leaders. She boldly entered the pope's palace and reminded him that the church's highest mission is that of saving souls. Catherine was used to bring justice and healing to a world besieged with corruption, violence, and the plague.

Henrietta Mears found her purpose. After accepting a position as Christian education director and moving to California in 1928, Henrietta took a 450-student Sunday school enrollment to an amazing 6,000 within three years.

Joni Eareckson Tada, after a tragic accident left her a quadriplegic, accepted God's purpose and is now known around the world for her Joni and Friends ministry. Her five-minute radio program is heard over 850 broadcast outlets and was named Program of the Year by the National Religious Broadcasters in 2002. She has authored over thirty books.

Preparing for My Purpose

Jeremiah 1:4, 5 tells us, "The word of the Lord came to me saying, 'Before I formed you in the womb I knew you, before you were born I set you apart; I appointed you as a prophet to the nations.'"

God had a purpose for Jeremiah and, likewise, he presents us with a purpose. When God calls us to our purpose, we enter a preparation period. This period prepares us with ministry information and spiritual maturity.

Often, once we accept our position we feel compelled to immediately enter our area of ministry. We skip the preparation. Some believe the process isn't necessary. Others maintain the preparation is too painful. Still others delay the process. Regardless of our stance, we must adequately prepare because a novice in the ministry is ineffective (see 1 Timothy 3:6). Let's consider the consequences of skipping preparation.

Have you encountered people who are dangerous behind the wheel? They may pass the road test, but they're not emotionally mature enough to handle the traffic. They're careless and take chances with others' lives. They fail to discern the seriousness of automobile safety.

Well-intentioned Christians who insist upon leadership positions before they receive adequate training have the ability to cause numerous problems. They bring much harm to the church as they misinterpret scripture, faint during times of adversity, and lack spiritual discernment. While leaders are not faultless, they are required to rise to a certain level of maturity that comes through the preparation process (see Titus 1:5-9).

Some avoid the preparation period. They want fresh strawberry cake but they'd rather somebody else pick the strawberries. A floral garden in their backyard is most desired, but they're not willing to till the soil. They aspire to have children who love God, but not if it means nightly devotions. A legal debate rings their bell, but no law school please. Large salaries appear impressive, but not if the road begins with a novice position. Teaching is cool, but learning isn't. Writing is cool, but sacrifice isn't. Preaching is cool, but dedication isn't. Doctors are cool, but education isn't. The preparation process requires something from us.

Maybe I'm a little wacky, but I enjoy the preparation process. Before becoming a pastor's wife or even knowing I would be one, I went into a preparation process. I worked in almost every area of the church. I taught classes for children, teens, women, and young married couples. I taught in every conceivable situation. I taught in small rooms, hot rooms, crowded rooms, noisy rooms, and the great outdoors. I've taught adults with children crawling on the table and adults sleeping beside it. I've heard every excuse that's ever been invented for lack of church attendance.

I've played the piano for teen and junior choirs and sung in the choir when they were desperate. I've worked with senior adults and shut-ins. I've cooked for crowds, performed multiple fund-raisers, and learned everything not to do. I've written skits and programs and decorated on low budgets. I've invented amazing creations out of paper, spray paint, and glue.

I've said on more than one occasion, "I'm never doing this again," especially while I cut out over a hundred gingerbread men out of one-inch-thick Styrofoam with a cookie cutter—almost impossible. And then I went on to cut hundreds of gold metallic stars from a papered poster board—my fingers numb. Then I hung them individually from a ceiling—all the while saying, "Why did I invent this ridiculous project?" But the sacrifice seemed but a pittance when I witnessed the delighted expressions from those attending the senior adult Christmas party.

The classes, the decorating, the choir, and the ministry helps were all a part of the preparation process to becoming a pastor's wife. Even waiting tables in a restaurant banquet hall served as preparation. The Bible study classes were preparation. I loved the preparation, which involved people, excitement, music, decorating, cooking, table setting, and even driving the church van.

As a writer and teacher, I've also enjoyed college, reading, study, and conferences. Researching in libraries and bookstores and on the Internet are some of my favorite hobbies. Difficult days happen to us all. But if our focus is correct, love for the calling and love for preparing can't be separated. The passion empowers us to overcome without being overwhelmed.

Mentors

Another important part of preparation for our ministry is mentoring. Mentors come alongside God to provide personal training for our ministry. God presented Samuel with Eli and David with Samuel. He gave Elisha the prophet Elijah and Timothy the apostle Paul. God provides mentors for us. Look around you. She's there and she'll prepare you in ways you never dreamed possible.

God blessed me with great mentors. Lorrie, a dear friend, is one of the most passionate women I've ever met. She possesses a great love for people and extends mercy to unheard-of extremes without complaint. Her daily actions model

God's love for man. I've witnessed her many tears for the hurting and seen her spend countless hours at the hospital consoling the sick. She taught me that ministry isn't limited to Sunday, but involves a lifestyle. I know how to love because she did first.

Aubrey, my former pastor, and his wife, Marion, modeled godliness. They opened their home on more than one occasion to others in need, for meals or even a temporary place to live. Marion knew the importance of involving people. Within a few weeks of attending the church, I received a phone call asking me to help serve a banquet. I was ecstatic. I felt I belonged. When my husband was hospitalized, she prepared a large container of homemade steak biscuits for our family. I have said many times that I want to bless others with the same attitude as she has blessed us.

My hometown pastor, Roger, mentored me from afar with his love for lost souls. His joy has been a light in my hometown for many years. His desire that the town come together to pray for the city has inspired others to want the same. He was the first person who encouraged my writing. I'm deeply thankful for his model of soul winning, encouragement, and joy.

If your mentor is in a successful position, she didn't arrive without great effort. She spent years gaining knowledge that you need to learn too. God placed her there for you.

We can be guilty of looking so far ahead that we can't enjoy the now—the process. Have you considered that if you can't enjoy the preparation period, the actual ministry may not be as fulfilling as you anticipate? Have you been guilty of criticizing your God-ordained mentor rather than gleaning knowledge from her? Have you felt alone in this process? Have you failed to look in your immediate surroundings for God's trainer? Your mentor may be sharing your bed.

My husband, Robert, not only encourages me, but also offers valuable advice in numerous areas. He is a wordsmith genius. He can spot a misused word or spelling error in a blink. His thirst for knowledge is inspiring and his dedication to the ministry uplifting. Integrity is foremost in his mind. His commitment toward excellence has brought me to a new level. I'll never settle for less.

Don't forget to surround yourself with greatness—people who are better educated, better groomed, and better conversationally. Look also for those who live life on a higher spiritual plane. They'll keep you stretching.

Maybe you require a slight boost in the right direction. Consider yourself supercharged. You're now ready to conquer unfamiliar territory. Begin this adventure with an open mind and determined spirit. You own a purpose. Go for it!

I Can Do Something About This

I can do everything through him who gives me strength
(Philippians 4:3)

Pray
Dearest Lord,
Thank you for another day where I can begin again.
I'll no longer waste the precious life you've given me.
Today I'm planting a seed into soil. I'm going to watch
it grow, even as I grow by taking these bold new steps.
I'm made for a purpose and I'm going to fulfill
my purpose, just as this seed fulfils its purpose.

Supplies
A packet of seeds—flowers or herbs
Small plastic pot
Small bag of dirt
Fertilizer (optional)
Water

Plant
Plant a seed according to the package directions.

Water
Water the seed according to the package directions.

Watch
Watch for growth to spring forth. Pray as you observe the plant. Pray for life to come forth in you. Pray for direction. Pray for hope.

THE WIND AND A CHILD

The wind and a child had a meeting one day,
And I was the only one saw it.

The wind kissed the child, then said, "Will you dance?"
And I was the only one saw it.

Wind and child, child and wind,
They danced their wild dance together.

Her hair streamed behind as her feet spun around
And I was the only one saw it.

She cried out with joy as she opened her arms.
And I was the only one saw it.

Child and wind, wind and child,
Two innocents dancing together.

The wind touched her face to tell her good-bye,
And I was the only one saw it.

The child now stood still with a smile on her lips
And I was the only one saw it.

The wind and a child had a meeting one day,
And I was the only one saw it.

—WANEDA BROWNLOW
1997—Bagheria, Sicily

Chapter

NINE

ନ୍ତ

Born to Fly

Soaring over
Interruptions

ନ୍ତ

URING A QUIET morning of devotions, the Holy Spirit impressed me with a thought: *Why do you walk when you can fly?* I pictured a bird as it hopped along the ground, refusing to use its wings. As I continued to pray, I realized much of my life centered on areas I personally managed. I rarely considered a giant leap of faith—except on those days when I felt spiritually supercharged within the safe confines of my home or church. Anything else was too scary and radical.

As I considered the question, I remembered a recent incident in the car. I drove down the interstate, caught up in worship, when the tape stopped. To no avail, I attempted to

147

release the tape from the player. I pushed the button and prayed at the same time, "Lord, you know this tape was blessing me. Please make it work again."

As I continued to punch the release button, the Lord answered, *Lisa, if you'd remove your finger from the button, I'd help you.* How could God receive glory? My fingers controlled all the switches. My actions were like swallowing an Excedrin® and asking God to heal my headache. What stopped the pain, God or the Excedrin?

When my fingers keep punching the buttons, it's what some people call "chopping wood with a dull ax." Others say it's "staying in the boat when we could walk on water," "paddling upstream against the current," "sailing against the wind," or planting strawberries in Virginia in December. It doesn't work. God interrupts us along the way and says, *Hello down there! This isn't that difficult! Here's what you need to do.*

Why walk when we can fly? Why indeed? Who wants to walk anywhere? We walk five miles inside the mall walkways, but fight for a parking space five feet from the outside entrance. Walking is good exercise. I purchased a pedometer and began taking ten thousand steps a day. I'm amazed at the times I fall far short of this goal. This partly comes because I spend many hours a day writing and researching. Even though I occasionally walk two miles, this doesn't help times of inactivity. I enjoy making creative efforts to achieve the ten thousand steps, such as walking inside of my house late at night doing what hyperactive children do to amuse themselves— flapping my arms like a bird, contorting my hips, marching army style, or bobbing my head. I'm even parking further away from the entrance. I need the exercise.

I know a place that provides numerous spaces at its entrances for senior adults. Does this mean all senior adults are handicapped? My seventy-six-year-old mother said, "I'm not parking in one. I need to walk."

"Mom, that's okay; you walk. But remember the special parking place on a rainy day or when you're experiencing a mentally rainy day or when your feet hurt or when you require pampering."

I didn't need to wait for her reply for I knew what it would be: "That's most any day of the week. I think I'll walk."

Walk Upright

We crawl before we walk, and so it is with flying. Consider the spiritual dynamics of walking. The Bible associates walking as being in close relationship with God. The Bible says Noah, Enoch, and Abraham walked upright before God (Genesis 5:24, 6:9, 17:1–3). We further explore Scripture to discover God invites us all to walk in his ways (Psalm 1:1, 119:1–3; Ephesians 4:2). We're all called to a life of walking upright before God.

> Who may ascend the hill of the LORD? Who may stand in his holy place? He who has clean hands and a pure heart, who does not lift up his soul to an idol or swear by what is false. He will receive blessing from the LORD and vindication from God his Savior (Psalm 24:3–5).

Walking with God is like achieving credentials necessary for flying. Walking upright earns us rewards. When God observed how Enoch walked with him, he took him to heaven. When God saw that Noah walked with him, he presented him a job building an ark. When Abraham received God's invitation to walk upright, God made an eternal covenant with him.

Congressman Jim Ryun tells the story of being a child and wanting to fly like Superman. He emptied items from his mother's refrigerator and spices from her cabinet into a glass. He felt if he drank the mixture, he'd fly. He swallowed part of the horrible concoction and attempted to fly without success. Then he thought if he drank the entire glass it would achieve the desired result. He drank the contents, but still couldn't fly.[1]

We want to accomplish the supernatural like Mr. Ryun. Flying takes us there. When we fly we soar into areas otherwise impossible. We see into a world normally hidden from us. Prayer takes us there.

Flying Takes Us Higher

Prayer transcends natural laws and connects us with God. With his assistance the impossible is possible. Last January such an event occurred. While in Virginia I drove my parents and niece to a restaurant to meet other members of our family for dinner. I didn't notice the stopped car in front of us. I quickly slammed on the brakes, but they locked up and the car began to skid because of the wet pavement. We braced ourselves for the impending crash, while I cried out, "Jesus! Lord Jesus!" My car came to an abrupt stop.

"What a prayer!" my mother said, laughing from the backseat.

"Lisa hit the curb!" my niece declared.

"No, she didn't hit a curb. She was nowhere near it," Mom said.

"Dad, what happened?"

"Sugar, I don't know, but something did."

Before bed, I attempted to write of the incident in my journal. I again approached my logical-thinking dad for his comments on the incident.

"Dad, did something supernatural happen in our car tonight?"

He shook his head and again replied, "I don't know what happened. I can't explain it." Neither could I.

What happened? As I reentered my room to attempt to describe the scene, these words rose in my heart. *At the mere mention of my name, I am there.* I began to cry.

"Oh Lord, I know you were there! I can't explain it. I don't know if you sent an angel to stop the crash. All I know is that you were there."

Prayer in Jesus' name transcends natural laws and soars us into the throne room of God. Prayer allows us to partner with him and to view the world from his perspective, which takes us higher.

While visiting a church member in the hospital, I noticed a clear view of the parking lot outside her window. I turned to her and said, "Don't you wish you had a megaphone to direct traffic down there?" From our location we easily saw that many cars lined up to enter the lot where no parking spaces existed. How often do we waste our time because of our inability to see around the corner? Not so with God.

God sees the whole picture. Sometimes, I wish he'd shout down the solution to satisfy my anxiety. Occasionally he does, but at other times I mysteriously ride the lot looking for a parking space. I cherish those wonderful moments when I'm in sync with him, like the Monday morning I prayed and Thelma came to mind.

The weekend before I had visited my family. While eating at my brother's restaurant, I saw an older lady from church whom I hadn't seen in a while. The sadness in Thelma's eyes broke my heart. Her husband had recently died.

After returning home on Monday, I remembered Thelma and her sadness. As she came to mind, the Lord lifted my heart with encouraging words. *I will make her eyes to shine again.* I felt the need to call her and share this. She was very kind and thanked me for sharing.

Two years passed before I spoke to Thelma again. She called to impart some wonderful news. "As I got ready to attend a church revival this evening, I passed a mirror in the hallway. At first what I saw startled me. My eyes sparkled. Immediately, I remembered your call several years ago. I knew I must tell you that it's true. God has made my eyes to shine again. I have met a wonderful man."

Months passed before I saw Thelma in person. When I did, she presented me with a wedding picture to keep as a memento of God's goodness to her. This picture serves as a treasured symbol of God's willingness to allow me to partner with him. This is how it feels to fly with God—exciting. He elevates me into places I can't explain. I enter into a relationship far better than companionship. I commune with God.

Ravi Zacharias says it like this:

In companionship with God we come to him, recognizing our limit of strength. In communion with God we stay with him, recognizing our depth of spirit. In companion-ship with God we long to see and understand. In commun-ion with God we long to feel and belong. Those who seek companionship without communion seek power without commitment, a display without dedication, and proof without love. [2]

What persuades a man to leave his lucrative law practice to relocate his family to Haiti? Why would a doctor do the same? What compels a princess to leave her palace for a grass hut to teach children from another culture about Jesus? God speaks and we're forever changed. The world declares we're utterly insane. Haven't they always? What does it matter if we're convinced God directs our steps?

Maybe you're afraid of hearing God. Maybe you think he'll ask you to sell your car and give the money to missions or buy someone lunch. He might. Unfortunately, you may never know. You're too attached to gazing into the sky and wondering what's waiting over the rainbow. You're not interested in messing up your hair or feeling gusts of wind toss your clothing. You'd rather miss the blessing of obedience than be inconvenienced.

Maybe heights frighten you and this is a ladder you'd rather not climb. You feel less secure, more vulnerable. You detest the notion of jumping and waiting for someone to catch you. You need full control. Knowing someone else is monitoring the control panel is frightening—like riding a roller coaster.

Just so you know, I intensely hate roller coasters. My last stint aboard one was over ten years ago. I finally said, "I'm a grown woman. I don't need to do this anymore." That declaration ended it. Maybe roller coasters unsettle me because I wonder if they're tempting God. Maybe I think they're too ungodly, and he wouldn't help me if the wheels jumped off the track. I'd rather be certain that the Lord would catch me in midair before my body splattered on the pavement.

Have you said no because this flying higher business seems too much like the roller coaster experience? Uncertainty grips your heart. You're not sure God will catch you if you fall. If these thoughts plague you, consider a change of theology. Trade your doubts for trust. Trusting God to follow *our* plans offers a questionable outcome, but trusting God to follow through on *his* plans always brings certainty.

When God calls us to fly higher with him, we know he'll not drop us. Although flying is a little scary at first, eventually we relax and trust the experience. We're certain of the Pilot's navigation skills. It's when we launch out on our own that we fish all night and catch nothing more than an old shoe.

I love the wind. Maybe this is why I enjoy flying. When the wind blows, I'm convinced God instructs it to blow solely for my sake. On our back porch, we have two wind chimes. When the bells tinkle, I know the wind is blowing and it does my heart good.

When we're airborne, we are stretched beyond our ability to produce. A magic potion didn't elevate us nor did several dozen balloons. Just like walking on the water, it's a God thing.

Flying Sets Us Free

When God says we must reach higher, we buck against him because we've settled for the familiar. We've decided that eating three meals a day at McDonald's is good enough. We've said that a pair of jeans, sweatshirt, and sneakers are appropriate gear for every occasion. We're happy with the same walk around the block. We don't want to explore a new trail. We're locked in—forever.

What if Abraham had refused to leave home because he liked his own bed, despised hotels and traveling, and felt he'd miss his friends? What if Noah had ignored God's request to build the ark because he feared persecution, and feared God wouldn't bring a flood? What if David had rejected the call to be king because he abhorred the responsibility? We should be glad for men who sculpted an image of faith to present to successive generations. They not only walked with God, they soared far into the heavens with him. We must do the same. Another generation follows. What model will we leave them to duplicate?

Steps toward obedience are like crawling. Babies aren't intended to perpetually crawl on their knees. College students don't remain in school. Caterpillars mustn't settle forever for a cocoon. Babies walk. Students graduate. Caterpillars evolve into beautiful butterflies and fly away. We must proceed likewise. We must fly.

The catalyst that's interrupting you is probably God nudging you out of your cage. You define it as a huge irritation. You fail to see God. Your focus is directed toward leaving home, losing friends, suffering persecution, added responsibilities, and an uncertain future. You fail to notice the ark that is protecting you in the storm. The excitement of traveling with God escapes you. The covenant God offers confounds you.

You're weary because you haven't moved to the next level. You're pressed into a mundane ritual. God is offering you a new pair of wings. Look for them. Isaiah 40:29–31 reminds us:

> He gives strength to the weary and increases the power of the weak. Even youths grow tired and weary, and young men stumble and fall; but those who hope in the LORD

will renew their strength. *They will soar on wings like eagles*;
they will run and not grow weary, they will walk and not
be faint (emphasis added).

As we put our trust in God, he lifts us above carnality.
The impossible suddenly seems possible. We discover God is
limitless. Cancer is not the end. Financial ruin isn't the final
answer. Relationships are healed. Souls receive Jesus. Wisdom
is certain and our future secure.

Grounded

We're soaring into the heavens. We observe life from a new
perspective. We wonder why we waited. Like children, we long
to eternally preserve this experience. But something clips our
wings and we quickly lose altitude. We're grounded again.
What happened? We grasp the art of flying, but we have yet
to master storm survival methods. This is a technical difficulty we'll eventually manage. It's essential that we be
momentarily grounded. We have additional lessons to learn.

Once grounded, we question God. "Are you in the small
stuff?" We accept that God is with Moses because he accom-
plishes the miraculous. We believe God is with Abraham
because he sets up a covenant with him for future generations. Yes, and David is important and so are Elijah, Daniel,
and Isaiah, but what about me?

I've discovered it isn't the big things that drown me in two
feet of water. When the tidal waves rush ashore, an internal
lifesaving mechanism kicks into gear. It tells me God is greater
and I easily acquiesce. Notwithstanding, people surround me
in the big issues. But it's the accumulation of seemingly
insignificant trifles that topples me over the edge. It's the tele-

phone conversation that causes me to run late for an important meeting. And then I spill coffee on my blouse before I exit
the house. I'm required to change the entire outfit because my
skirt doesn't match anything else in the closet. Then the cell
phone rings: "Where are you?" As I hurry off in my car, I see
colorful lights flashing in my rearview mirror and get a
speeding ticket. The phone rings again—my child is sick and
I need to pick him up at school. This can't be happening.

The day doesn't get better for me. Because of my absence
at the meeting I'm handed a list of work to complete—an
assignment due the following Monday. Impossible! Before I
leave, a call comes through to inform me of unexpected company. This week, in addition to three church functions, I have
spots on my carpet, a weed-infested flowerbed, bushy bushes,
and leaf-strewn walkways—and my entire household is out
of underwear.

The older I get, the more these things seem to happen to
me. I say to myself, "You big sissy. What a wimp. So what if
my house is a mess when the company arrives? They just
won't come back, and won't I be glad? But then they'll tell all
my friends what a slob I am." So I compromise with what I
can and cannot live with—a little dirt is okay but nastiness
is out of the question.

I dust around the figurines, dump bleach in the toilet and
down the sink drains. Then I quickly mop the bathroom
floor with a washcloth. I end it by shoving everything into
the office closet. What about sheets—clean or not? Clean.
Because I believe in doing unto others what I would like done
unto me. Clean sheets.

I live in Florida. During the 2005 hurricane season, we
endured two threats and lived through two realities. In addition to the terrible storms, three virus Trojan horses forced

their way into my computer system. These events delayed my work on this book for numerous days. At the tail end of the hurricanes and after the third day of warring against Trojan horses, I had had enough.

I laid hands on the computer; no, not to throw it out the window. But I laid hands on the computer and prayed to God. Within thirty minutes, not only was I able to access the computer, but rid it of the final Trojan horse. I could do nothing but praise the Lord.

Why does the small stuff send us into a state of panic? Perhaps because of possible embarrassment. We cringe at the thought of appearing like an idiot. We desire respect from our colleagues. We want others to believe we disown dandruff, stinky feet, and underarm perspiration stains. This saving face business has us walking on a ridiculous high wire.

Daily, I'm expanding my vocabulary by minute increments. I've learned to say things such as; "I'm sorry. I was wrong. I have no excuse for being late. I should develop better time management skills. It's not the train's fault, the police officer's fault, the telephone's fault, or the coffee's fault that I'm late. I should have started earlier." Furthermore, I'm learning to say, "I can't complete the work in the time allotted. I don't want to inconvenience you, but I request more time." I can tell others, "My shoes are stored in my garage for a reason. You don't want me to take mine off in your house." What keeps me airborne is the revelation that God values me. When I lose sight of this I'm grounded. When I demand approval from others, I'm grounded. When I measure myself against my peers, this grounds me. When I expect more from myself than I can complete, this grounds me. As I continue to focus upon the destination God points toward, I'm elevated. I'm going places, but where?

Our Destination

Birds instinctively understand the flight plan. Pilots charter a given course. Even airline passengers possess a desired destination. Where are they going? They know, but do we? Do we have a sense of purpose, or is the summation of our actions a hit-and-miss proposition? Ask God.

How do we know when God speaks and when he doesn't speak? How did Billy Graham determine God's desire for him as an evangelist or Ronald Reagan the call to the presidency or Bill Bright to Campus Crusade for Christ or Pat Robertson to the 700 Club? Isn't God's voice the same voice that spoke to Samuel to anoint David as king (1 Samuel 16:1-13)? And the same voice that nudged Anna toward the baby Jesus (Luke 2:36–38)? And the same voice that Paul, John, Peter, and countless other disciples obeyed?

Jesus tells us the sheep know the shepherd's voice (John 10:4, 5). Do we know his voice? Are we listening for his instructions? What is he telling us to do? Are we doing it? Are we flying?

No one is required to tell us we're flying. We instinctively know. We know when our purpose is revealed because we're basking in the freedom it brings. Once we encounter this mode of transportation, it's impossible to return. We might suffer a momentary lapse, like the small stuff business. But walk when we can fly? Never. Give me a mixer over a hand beater, a computer over a typewriter, and a mower that can gobble up three acres of grass without thinking. Who wants to push the powerless variety in a hundred degree weather? Who wants to walk when she can soar on the wings of the Spirit? Who wants to accomplish little when she can accomplish much with God?

Since the inception of this book, I've felt an overwhelming dependence upon God. Daily I pray for direction, insight, and inspiration. I realize I cannot do this without him, nor do I desire to complete this task without him. What purpose would this book serve without his divine assistance?

When I submit to take the hand of God to soar into places outside of my ability to reach, it's no longer about me. When I'm flying, I'm accomplishing his will. I can think of nothing more exciting than to be going places with God. I'm amazed with his flowing commentary concerning the world around me.

The night after my husband was buried, I awoke and went into my mother's family room to sit. I reflected upon the first time Steve visited Bermuda. He came back with pictures and great stories of its beauty. "You must come with me. The water is clear and blue. The fish are bright and colorful—some the color of a carrot, and others like the eye of a peacock feather. You must see the Bermuda longtail and the bright red poinciana tree and the passionflower and the fuchsia hibiscus growing by the roadside. The air is fresh and clean. The lifestyle is slow and relaxed. Family is important. They're not obsessed with television as Americans are. When you come, we can sit on the cliff and watch the sunset and ride our mopeds around the island. We can snorkel and helmet dive and kiss on our own private beach. We can eat fish at my favorite restaurant. You'll love it." And one day I did. It was more than I imagined.

As I recalled his enthusiasm and compelling visuals, it occurred to me he was still telling me these things. "Lisa, heaven is bright and beautiful. You'll not believe the sparkling streets of gold nor the gates of pearl nor the greenness of the grass and trees nor the variety of colors in your favorite shades of pinks, reds, blues, and greens. You must come."

Won't you come with me now? Won't you give your heart, your mind, your soul, your strength to Christ? Won't you surrender each heartache to him? Won't you mount up on wings as eagles and give Jesus a chance? You won't be sorry. Too many people have gone before us. They've sent word that the view is great. We can't miss it. This is the only life we own. With every breath it's evaporating. Like an arrow released from a bow, it lands quickly and then it's over.

One day I'll be soaring through the sky and I'll receive this nice surprise. God will take my hand and he'll keep taking me higher. I'll continue to rise until I reach my ultimate destination—heaven. All the sacrifices made on earth will pale in comparison to the loveliness surrounding me. Upon beholding its beauty, I'll wish I had convinced more to come with me.

"The Spirit and the bride say, 'Come!' And let him who hears say, 'Come!' Whoever is thirsty, let him come; and whoever wishes, let him take the free gift of the water of life" (Revelation 22:17).

I Can Do Something About This

I can do everything through him who gives me strength
(Philippians 4:3)

Pray
Dearest Lord,
I admit that the thought of flying is a bit scary,
even if exciting. I'm not certain what this will require of me.
But I'm willing to surrender my reservations and to continue
forward with you. I want to fulfill my purpose and I don't
want to meet you in heaven with nothing to lay before you.
I trust you to lead me where your grace will keep me.

Accept
Ask God what he is calling you to do and accept it.

Question
What do I need to do to prepare myself
to do as God requests?

Prepare
Make a list of all areas of preparation.

Organize
Prioritize this list.

Set
Study your preparation list and place a realistic
completion date next to each item.

Ask

Designate a friend to make you accountable to accomplish each goal. This friend will call you at designated intervals to inquire about your progress and to celebrate with you with every success and to encourage you with every defeat.

GRACE COMES QUICKLY

Interrupted by grace one day
When mostly, life seemed bleak.
Having tried living the worldly way,
Knew I needed to hear God speak.
So I bowed head and heart,
And asked him to COME.
He came quickly.

"My grace is sufficient for you," he said.
"Stop striving. Let go. Follow me."
For you are My child, and you need to know
That My Son and His gift set you free!
As I felt spirit lift, and saw hope take wing,
True freedom invaded my soul.
He comes quickly.

Divine interruptions help us to grow,
If we're open, desiring His best.
Through us, grace teaches others to know
Interruptions are part of His test.
They come quickly.

He'll never fail. He wants us to call.
He loves being needed. He's given His all.
His touch is only a whisper away.
He's listening and waiting—to hear us say,
Come quickly.

Be available, flexible, use His hands and heart.
Show His love and His truth and grace.
A simple response, to pray, do our part
Can light up our Master's face.
Now it's our turn—Go quickly!

—CHERYL JOHNSTON

CEO and Christ
Successfully
Interrupted

THOUGHTS OF success interrupt us daily. Are we successful? What determines success? Our ideas of success come packaged in various designs. For many, success is wrapped up in the sensation that one is the best, one owns the best, or one imitates the best.

Success lends us great respect. Success communicates phrases such as:

> "I'm a part of the action."
> "I'm where it's happening."
> "I have the inside scoop."
> "I'm on top of the world."
> "I'm somebody."

We're created to accomplish goals, strive for excellence, and improve our living conditions. But we can't confuse advancement with an insatiable desire to be the best. If we seek always to be the best, eventually we'll communicate the message we're better than others.

We're the Best

As a child, King of the Mountain was a fun game (when I was king), even if that meant my younger sister was residing in the ditch. In school, we held contests to see who was the best speller or math student or who was the fastest or strongest. Like most, I aspired to be them all.

Our competitive nature urges us to desire the upper class position, the most popular, the most beautiful, the most admired, and to be the best athlete, skater, pianist, vocalist, actress, dancer, student, or artist.

As parents, we believe our children must be the best. After all, they uttered their first words before the English language was invented. Their first step stunned the neighborhood and their first tooth made the *Guinness Book of World Records*. Where a mother will eventually concede to the better party, a grandmother never will. She'll offer a polite smile and listen as you rattle on, but when you take a breath she'll insert, "If you think that's something, you should see my grandbaby."

Our definitions of success plague us for a lifetime. If we're not a cheerleader or the Cotton Queen, we've failed. If the most popular guy doesn't present us a passing glance, we've failed. If we didn't graduate with a special sash indicating academic achievement, we've failed. We feel inadequate if our income doesn't reach a pre-determined level. We sink deeper in the mire if we're not attractive enough or our home fancy enough or our children smart enough, athletic enough, or spiritual enough.

If others didn't recognize our work, we've failed. If we made a mistake, we've forever failed. We continue through life with a huge "F" emblazoned on our chest. We wonder how a little healthy competition became a mark of failure from which we never rid ourselves.

I fared far better when I built mud cakes in the sandbox, created angels in the snow, and erected houses out of playing cards. The trouble came when my cakes, my angels, and my houses had to be better than everybody else's. It was like an endless Olympic race that nobody wins.

Our ideology is askew when we convince ourselves we must be the leader in every situation. We have one president in this country. Does this indicate failure for the rest of us? We have one CEO of the company. Does this say everyone else in the company is a failure? We have one boss in our immediate work area, one teacher in the classroom, one pastor of the church. Still, success comes to us all—when we learn to correctly define our position in life.

The competitive journey is endless and sometimes leads us into the areas we least expect to be. We may find ourselves so caught up in winning that it includes areas such as who had the worst day, the worst experience, the worst illness, the worst husband, or the worst haircut. From here we travel on to who has the busiest schedule, heaviest burden, sickest parent, and messiest house. He who owns the worst, busiest, heaviest, sickest, and messiest is crowned with the black laurel wreath.

Decide today to extricate yourself from the competition trap. Begin by defining success for yourself. Understand that it's okay if you're not the town beauty, the most intelligent, or the most athletic. You may be married to a blue-collar worker and struggle to pay your bills. You may not own everything you'd like, but that doesn't mean you're not successful.

Releasing the grip of competition in no way releases us from achieving necessary goals. We simply must learn to compete against ourselves rather than others. I'm an avid reader. I've determined each year to read more books than the year before. I also extend this to Bible study, Scripture memorization, work hours, family time, educational classes, weight loss, and so on. I'm always seeking to stretch myself in new dimensions.

My achievements arrive incrementally. I've learned to resist huge leaps unless I feel impressed by God to make them. These conclusions regarding the interruption of competition came through a series of events beginning in my teens.

A Struggle to Discover Success

When I was sixteen, my teacher felt I should enter a competition to become a state officer for our club. I asked, "What do I have to do?" He said, "Write a speech and deliver it at the state convention." It seemed like an interesting challenge, so I agreed.

Our school sent nine students to the convention. When we arrived at the historic big city hotel, the striped silk drapery in the lobby, the enormous sparkling crystal chandeliers, the tapestried carpet, and the large ornate antique furnishings enamored me. I'd never before witnessed such elegance.

Soon after our arrival I discovered I'd have a campaign booth. Great! My own campaign booth! I felt like *somebody*. I was on my way to presidency. But the excitement soon faded when I spied my two competitors' booths.

Their booths displayed massive professionally printed patriotic posters with their pictures printed on the front. Campaign representatives were behind each counter wearing T-shirts bearing the candidate's image. They handed out free campaign pencils and badges to each passersby. I had nothing. My teacher was new to this process of election. He wasn't aware such paraphernalia was necessary. But my loving school friends rectified his oversight.

They went to the store, purchased markers and posters, and made huge ugly signs that proved we were country bumpkins in the big city. Even though I appeared ridiculous in the whole setting, the gift of love extended from my friends helped erase the embarrassment.

The night before the speech, my teacher asked me to rehearse for him. I felt confident, though nervous, because of my extreme familiarity with what I wanted to say. I recited and then waited proudly for his comment. He said, "Good, but you didn't say . . ." I panicked and wondered if it was possible to make the necessary changes at this late hour. Nevertheless, I stayed up into the early hours of the morning in an attempt to rememorize the speech.

The next day arrived soon enough. I dressed in my favorite peach-colored pantsuit and cream blouse. If I were to be defeated, I'd be a finely dressed loser. Dripping in perspiration, I stood behind the podium, feeling the heat of hives travel the length of my neck. My brother said my hives look like a horror film where an evil red hand comes from behind and wraps itself up my neck and slowly creeps along the side of my face.

As I continued to stand on the platform, the audience transformed into the customers I served in the family-style restaurant. These people weren't strangers. An easy smile illuminated my face. I gave it my all and sat down.

The audience cast their vote and we waited. I felt certain my female opponent had won. She possessed the most impressive campaign gear and held an excellent academic resume. Seeing no other way, I prepared myself for defeat. The area teacher supervisor walked onto stage with a smile on his face and a piece of paper in his hand.

He walked behind the stand and announced the winner—Lisa Marie Sheetz. After a moment of stunned silence, our country bumpkin group went wild.

Afterward, the supervisor said, "Lisa, I candidly confess I didn't think you stood a chance. The other candidates underestimated the consequences of delivering a written speech. Your memorized speech won it for you."

Through the years I've pondered his statement. The supervisor thought he had witnessed failure when he beheld crude drawings on pieces of poster board. I don't blame him because I looked around and saw the same. But my teacher understood more than us all. He envisioned a giant S emblazoned on my chest—success. He believed in me.

When I was even younger, a junior high school guidance counselor invited me into her office for an annual evaluation. She asked me what I wanted to be someday. I told her I wanted to be a model. She studied me for a moment and said, "I notice you wear a particular outfit quite often. You have a wonderful talent with colors, but you wear this outfit several times a week that indicates to me you are from a family with inadequate funds. I suggest you reconsider your dream, because you need money to pursue a modeling career."

I left her office confused and crushed. I didn't know how to process her evaluation. I recognized her concern and even her support, but the haunting feeling that she was watching me and found a missing ingredient plagued me for many years. Yet, a burning passion kindled that wanted to prove her assessment wrong.

Four years later when my role as a state representative was complete, I met a woman, Jackie, from New York who asked if I would be her model for a hair show. This began a relationship that eventually led me to New York and into the offices of the two top modeling agencies in the world. People at both agencies liked my looks. Unbelievable. But I never went back. All I wanted to know was that the guidance counselor was wrong about me.

All sorts of people enter my life at different points, and each carry labels they seek to attach to my forehead and heart. I have to make either conscious or unconscious decisions concerning their evaluations. Success begins in the positive relationship with people who believe I have the potential for greatness, not those who glance my way and render hasty judgments. I need the encouragement from these positive relationships. It's like gas in my tank; like the fuel surge I receive from my husband Robert.

Since Robert's first spouse had died, I felt he would understand if I shared moments of deepest emotional anguish over Steve's death. While we were dating I shared my precious journals, which I'd never disclosed with another. He responded with vigor: "You described my feelings in vivid detail." He validated not only my right to hurt, but also my ability to express it. His repeated affirmations empowered me to write this book—a task I would have otherwise never felt talented enough to accomplish. Affirmation isn't the only benefit of success.

Success Costs Us

For some, success is merely an unattainable dream because strong illusions of grandeur cast a cloud over reality. We dream of winning the Miss America title and when that isn't achievable, we attempt the mental picture of fitting a body that's birthed three babies into a Mrs. America swimsuit. Even when we realize the absurdity of this wasted vision, we dream on way past our years of possible achievement. We can't fix our deception over success because success isn't what we dream but what we attain. This failure costs something important to us every day—precious time.

As life would have it, if these unfulfilled dreams continue, they spill over into our senior years where we eventually find ourselves in a calico-printed cotton duster, white haired, dimmed vision, rocking on the porch, and reading romance novels, *TV Guide, People*, and *Soap Opera Digest*—all as we gossip about the neighbor's activities while sipping from a glass of iced tea. Life can be empty.

My oldest brother, Darrell, spent many of his years working odd jobs to pay the bills. But then one day with the help of his wife, Donna, he locked into his passion—computers and electronic technology. At forty years of age, he decided to attend college to earn his degree. Not only did he find his passion; he also determined to fulfill it. But there was a large cost involved. It wasn't easy to go back to school and work another job. He struggled with time constraints, renewing his study skills, and finances. But he did it and I'm very proud of his accomplishment.

Still Defining Success

As I became a young woman, I continued to struggle to define success. Like many, I thought marriage to a rich man would solve this problem. While at dinner one evening, a friend introduced me to a tall handsome man who had recently graduated from law school. He asked if I would accept his phone call. Of course, I said YES!

The next day he arrived at my place of work with his brother and sister. When he came into view, I presented my biggest dumb blonde smile as I bounced across the store with my arms outstretched, "Hello, Rick!" His face fell and his siblings concealed laughter with their hands. *Oh no, what have I done.* His name wasn't Rick.

I didn't see him again for several years until I ran into him at a local fast-food restaurant. He sat by the window as he ate lunch with his mother. We smiled at each other as he stood to introduce her. He said, "Mom, this is Sheila. That is your name, Sheila?" I smiled and greeted her but ignored his jab. I was Sheila for that moment. So the rich man was out of the equation. I'd have to make my own strides toward success.

Magazines have us to believe success is contained in the tightness of our abs, the size of our breasts, and the shape of our rear. While the workout to achieve this has merit, the clothing worn the following day to buy groceries requires further evaluation. Once, we thought sensual apparel belonged in the bedroom, but now some women feel great pride in their bodies and long to display it to members of the opposite sex. Their husbands are satisfied with this arrangement because, like King Ahauserus, it boosts their ego to have men to lust after their Queen Vashti. "Lust, but don't touch. She's mine."

Once I felt the need to firm up. My neighbor and I attended aerobics three times a week. I was fit and firm, even with my triple chocolate cheesecake treat after class. Now it's laughable to think that I never felt slim in my twenty-five-pound-lighter-than-today body. Oh to be that size again. I was skinny. But success doesn't ride on our hips; it rests in our hearts.

We Own the Best

My search for success continued with drives around the afflu-
ent areas of town to admire the houses with enormous round
columns stretched across a porch bigger than my entire parent's house. I enjoyed the sculptured front yards, running
fountains, vine-covered gazebos, and massive entryways. I
especially liked the circular drive and imagined myself exit-
ing a limo before the driver pulled around back. I envisioned
every day as a grand entrance. I didn't realize rich folk entered
their back door just like I did.

One of my friends would say, "One day, I'm going to live in
that house." And I would try to outdo her by saying, "One day,
I'm going to live in the house toward the end of the street."
It was great fun to dream. We believed this was success—to
own a big house. But soon enough the reality of debt, taxes,
and maintenance bills dispelled those dreams.

As kids we desired all the things our girlfriends owned. If
she had a purple bicycle, we needed one. If she had the latest
Barbie, we needed one. If she had a red purse and shoes, we
had to own the same. We browsed the JC Penney Christmas
catalog and dreamed of all the toys we'd like piled in our
closet. If we owned those toys, we not only would be happy,
but we knew we would be the talk of the neighborhood kids.

As adults, nothing changes. They're just different kinds
of toys. For example, after my kitchen cabinets refused to
budge another inch, so did I. After all, how many appliances
do we need to mix, slice, dice, bake, broil, grill, steam, and
fry? I went on strike when my bakeware company added a
new color. I said no, brown will be okay. Through the years,
I rebelled against the mulberry, green, blue, gold, and red
insanity. I had a few rough moments when the mulberry

made its debut, but I took a few aspirins and chilled out. I got over it.

Chasing success is like a police pursuit that never catches the offender. We're never rid of our enemy. He hides from us and deceives us into believing he's in places he can't be found.

We Imitate the Best

If we can't be the best or own the best, we imitate the best.

We can't have leather seats, so we settle for vinyl.
We can't have Waterford, so we settle for glass.
We can't have silk, so we settle for polyester.
We can't have mahogany, so we settle for pressed board.
We can't have diamonds, so we settle for cubic zirconia.
We can't have hardback, so we settle for paperback.
We can't have long, healthy nails, so we settle for artificial.
We can't have marble, so we settle for plastic.
We can't have 14-karat gold, so we settle for fashion jewelry.
We can't have hand-sewn quilts, so we settle for manufactured ones.
We can't have home-cooked meals, so we settle for fast food.
We can't have Saks Fifth Avenue, so we settle for Wal-Mart.
We can't have the real potatoes, so we settle for instant.
We can't have Oxford, so we settle for the community college.

I can say these things because I've been there and still am. My winter coats aren't mohair or cashmere. Some of my jewelry is fake. I enjoy shopping at Wal-Mart. I once attended a community college. I've used instant potatoes when the real ones took too much time to boil. But, I must confess, nothing sparkles better than Waterford, or feels like silk, or smells like leather, or wears like hardback, or cleans like marble, or tastes like home-cooked, or sounds like education, or looks like hand-sewn.

So it is with God. We've learned to live with imitations. If we don't know the real, we don't know what we're missing. But if we've tasted the real, we know when something is missing. We've settled for sawdust when we can have gold dust. We may find it necessary to settle for glass rather than crystal, but we never need to settle for less than God. Some of us, however, are unaware of our lack.

> We've settled for losses when we could be winners.
> We've settled for lust when we could have love.
> We've settled for passivity when we could have peace.
> We've settled for pleasure when we could have joy.
> We've settled for suicide when we could have hope.
> We've settled for idols when we could have Jesus.
> We've settled for a house when we could have a home.
> We've settled for earth when we could have heaven.

Sometimes I wonder about our choices when I see stressed-out moms screaming at their children and husbands. Have we settled for less? Have we opted for a career label rather than the greatest label of all—Mom? Have we fooled ourselves into believing our children are better with fancier clothes, homes, and toys than a mother who has peace? A mother who rises early to pray? A mother who has time for fun? A mother who reads bedtime stories? Is any sacrifice too great for our children?

In the following letter to my son, I share some of my innermost feelings about our values.

Dear Joe,

I'm glad for all the nightly prayer meetings, bedtime stories, Scripture contests, and afternoon lunches—we've had some awesome conversations. I'll never tell. May you share secrets with your children.

I remember the time when you were a teenager and we turned up the music and listened to "Stomp" as we ran through the house dancing like crazy people. May your children think you're wild and crazy too.

Do you remember the personal revivals in the car— where we rewound the tape repeatedly and circled the block a dozen times? Sharing God with you felt good.

Thanks for the many times you asked my opinion. I can't describe how that has made me feel.

Yes, it was me making all those loud clapping noises and strangled wolf whistles when you won the coveted Eagle award, the marble-shooting contest, and all the sports honors. I'm so-o-o-o-o-o-o-o-o proud of you.

I'm glad you're waiting for the right girl. Sometimes, I can hardly wait to see her and share her interests. I've prayed for her for a long time now. You'll make a fine husband— just like your dad and stepfather.

Thanks for calling just to say hello. You'll always be my dear friend.

I cherish every moment you are home because, as God designed, one day things will change and you'll desire your own easy chair complete with remote control.

But when you look back, remember Barnes and Noble, books, and frappacinos, and share a smile with me.

Much, much, much, much love,
Mom

What Is Success?

When I didn't marry into wealth, didn't own a big house, and didn't possess fame I found that I needed to redefine success. What I discovered forever changed me. When I no longer sought after success, it found me in unexpected places.

Success came in the form of love—Steve and Joe in a little house in Virginia. Success grew as we fished, dreamed, shared, laughed, cried, and traveled together. Success continued to stand with me as I discovered my purpose, planned for my purpose, and lived out my purpose. Success met me in family and friends through the shared sorrow of death. Success is a happy home.

But most of all, success found me in Christ. It was in Christ I finally realized all the wood, hay, and stubble in my life. Homes perish. I live in Florida. I know. A big puff of wind will reduce them from a twenty-five foot pedestal into a two-foot-high pile of rubble. All that's within the shattered house perishes too—the bakeware, the Waterford crystal, the silk, the diamonds, and the Creative Memories albums.

Success meets you when you enter life fully understanding that it's not about being better than others, not about material wealth, not about positions, not about abs or butts or firm breasts. It's not about always being right, being the boss, and being smart.

Success is about love—creating it again and again with God's redemptive powers. Success is about happy memories that even a pair of Sears vise grips can't pry loose. Success is giving your best even when, to others, your best isn't good enough. Success is walking in the realization that life is a precious fleeting gift. We blink and it's gone.

Success is a friend, warm and welcoming, honest and confident. Dependable and never expendable—much like Jesus, my friend.

I Can Do Something About This

I can do everything through him who gives me strength
(Philippians 4:13)

Pray

Dearest Lord,
I desire to be free from the competition trap. In order to
do this, I must release my expectations and the expectations of oth-
ers and allow you to define success for me. I submit
feelings of unworthiness to you now. I long to be successful
and I know I can do this with your help.

Locate

Thumb through your King James Bible index
and locate words such as blessed, glad, and prosper.

Look

Look up these scriptures.

Write

Write them in a tablet and meditate on them.

Take

Take one of the shortest, most meaningful scriptures and
print it as small as possible on a separate sheet of paper.

Glue

Glue this scripture to the back side of a ribbon.

Tie
Tie the ribbon in a bow around your wrist.

Remember
Remember throughout the day that you're successful.

Share
Share with someone why you're successful.

He ate and drank the precious words,
His spirit grew robust;
He knew no more that he was poor,
Nor that his frame was dust.
He danced along the dingy days,
And this bequest of wings
Was but a book. What liberty
A loosened spirit brings!

—EMILY DICKINSON[1]

Chapter
ELEVEN

Coconut Head
Joyful Interruptions

AFTER STEVE DIED, Joe and I sat on the front pew at church. He was nine years old and I wanted him to love church, so I provided various games to make church fun. Sometimes he listened for certain words in the sermon, sometimes he drew a picture of the speaker's message, and other times he wrote down the verses the pastor mentioned. On this particular Sunday evening, his friend Billy sat with him.

The choir sang, the offering was taken, and our pastor was in the middle of an interesting message. Our eyes watched as he preached, darting back and forth across the platform until he finally came down the stairs into the altar area. To our astonishment as he reached the bottom step, he fell—within two feet of Joe and Billy. Their eyes widened and their hands flew to their mouths as he quickly returned to his feet. After a brief pause, he looked at the two boys and said, "Okay, you can laugh now." We all laughed and laughed until we couldn't stop. A mental picture of his fall and quick return to his feet replayed itself repeatedly in my mind.

As his message continued, so did my uncontrollable laughter. Each time I felt sufficiently recovered, upon glancing upward the giggles surfaced again. The embarrassment grew with the realization I couldn't absent myself without gaining attention. My face radiated the shade of a rose in my garden. Joe, having regained his composure, cast a "my mother is weird" look at me.

What's so funny? Don't ask a child. Ask me. If it's happened, it's happened to me. Like tumbling over store displays, blackening my eye while opening the car door, and knocking a lady to the floor in exercise class. Don't stand next to me.

I've learned much in my short forty-three years—such as don't walk around the bedroom brushing your teeth, lest an unexpected sneeze grips you. It's a real mess. Other lessons include:

Listen when instinct tells you to remove the red nail polish from the medicine cabinet. If you don't, it will fall on your tiled floor and dry quicker than it does on your fingernails. Not a semblance of a bottle will remain. The polish will crawl into every conceivable crevice—your grout, your drains, your wallpaper seams, and your best rugs. You will never forget it because you will clean red dots for the rest of your life.

Always keep a spare set of keys in your purse, because the car wash attendant has your number and he'll accuse you for the third time of locking your keys in the car. Which reminds me to further warn you not to leave your car running to attend a two-hour ladies' function. It's a waste of gas.

Keep your hands away from the beaters when whipping frosting. You might drive your finger through. That really hurts.

Remember where you parked lest the security guard decides not to take you around the parking lot again, but proceeds to the mental hospital.

Don't look for the building you're going to. Stay focused on the road or you'll hit the car directly in front of you.

Don't be fooled. Your mother's dog knows you don't like him. Beware while you're visiting her, for he's doing a thorough investigation of the entire nine-room house, and he knows the room you're sleeping in.

Please don't believe that others think you're funny when you do crazy things. They think you're stupid. Ask your family.

◎◎

When Joe was four years old we were in our hometown visiting family for the weekend. We attended church with my mother-in-law. I escorted Joe to his Sunday school class and left. After church his cousins rushed to me to share what Joe said in class.

Lee, his teacher, thought he recognized me and asked Joe my name. He replied, "Mama."

Lee said, "Yes, she's Mama, but what's her first name?"

Again he said, "Mama."

The teacher realized he needed to rephrase the question, so he said, "What does your daddy call your mama?"

"Coconut Head."

When you're nicknamed Coconut Head, you're up for grabs. When Joe was a teenager, he would fill the car with his friends and imitate my driving. To do this, he would erratically push the accelerator pedal and then stop suddenly. Then he'd lay his foot on the pedal for a quick takeoff—all the while banging his hand on the steering wheel as if he were having a wonderful conversation with himself.

Upon hearing this, my stepdaughter, Latese, laughed loudly. "I don't do that!" I protested.

"Yes, you do," she giggled.

Not much has changed through the years. I'm remarried now and along with this marriage came a precious grandson, Noah. When he was four, he spent his second weekend with us. While I stood on the other side of the kitchen counter, Noah said, "This is my right hand and this is my left." He was wrong. I unsuccessfully attempted to correct him from my side of the counter. Realizing my mistake, I went to the other side of the counter to stand beside him to explain. He looked at me and gave an exasperated sigh, "That's what I said!"

The following Monday Noah shared with his mother what we did over the weekend. He was confused concerning the location of the place we swam and his mother attempted to correct him by saying, "Your Nana Lisa said you went swimming in the nearby pool." He responded, "Oh, Mom, you can't listen to her. She doesn't know her right hand from her left hand."

Please don't tell my secrets. I want your family and friends to think somebody intelligent wrote this book.

Choose Joy

Since joy is what I choose, where is it? I can't find joy hiding behind a bush. I can't find it peeking out from under the amusement park carousel. It's not neatly wrapped in pretty paper under my Christmas tree. I can't locate it on the Disney Channel, *Saturday Night Live*, or prime-time TV. Joy lives inside me.

Because Jesus is the author of this joy, I carry it with me as I walk the aisles of the grocery store. It's there as I wait in line at the deli department, meat department, and fish department and even as I attempt to locate a man from produce to discover what happened to the bananas. But it slowly dissipates as I stand in line at the checkout. I look over at the other customers quickly paying for their purchases. I'm tempted to move into the next lane, but the past comes back to haunt me. *Lisa, as sure as you do, this lane will start moving. Don't do it.* I stood in line for an Olympic world record of thirty minutes. But I left thankful I didn't have ice cream.

Why am I laughing today at what drove me crazy the week before? I turned my head when the inconsiderate lady broke line. I chose to excuse her. I refused to look at my agenda and determined to focus on people and opportunities to make new acquaintances. I looked at the traffic jam that I couldn't possibly change and praised God for another moment spent alone with him. I allowed joy to seep through my pores like perspiration on a hot day—not to irritate but to cool my skin.

Like hyperactive children, I have fun with myself. I hold great private conversations, invent neat gadgets, and dream of feats I'll never accomplish. During these block-outs, I journey near and far. Some say, "Where do you go?" I say, "Anywhere but here." With the exception of a few minor embarrassments, these trips are fairly inexpensive.

The embarrassing part enters when I exit a conversation with really important people only to enter it with a statement previously made by another party—mostly my husband. In private, he'll jerk me in line by saying, "Lisa, you must start paying attention. Think about what you're doing. Do you realize how rude your actions appear to others? Think."

As always, I'll feel terrible and promise to do better next time. But then next time seems to fail me too. I talk to myself. *Think. Lisa. Think before you file these papers. Think. Think of the money you'll receive with next year's tax return.* Without fail I didn't think and the file disappeared. Don't ask me where it went. You know, it's impossible to think what people want you to think all the time.

One day driving home after church, I mentally rehearsed the morning's events—the teaching, preaching, singing, praying, and fellowship. As my thoughts wandered so did the vehicle, as if it had a mind of its own. Upon returning to earth, I found myself in a neighborhood I'd never seen before. *Oh where am I?* Panic seized me as I drove for what seemed an eternity to find a recognizable street. But today all is well. I don't feel as badly as I once did about mental vacations after reading Martha Bolton's *The Thinkers' Bill of Rights:*

> Thinkers don't worry about what other people might say. They know their thinking is important work. It might change the whole world. Or at very least their world. They give themselves permission to think because they know they have to do it to live. Thinkers are driven. They're committed. But the world doesn't always afford them their thinking space. That's why I believe thinkers need their own Bill of Rights.
>
> A thinker shall have the right to drive his or her car in the fast lane of the freeway with the left turn signal blinking.
>
> A thinker shall have the right to stare at the vegetables in the grocery store for prolonged periods of time without disturbance.
>
> A thinker shall have the right to ponder the greenness of the *go* light for a minimum of five seconds before venturing out into the intersection.

A thinker shall have the right to stare at his or her own belly button for as long as it takes to come up with the answers to life's most difficult questions.

A thinker shall have the right to stand and defend his or her right to think. Or to go home and sleep on it, whichever seems more inviting at the time.[2]

Love Brings Joy

I enjoy praying for extended periods of time. Almost twenty years ago when I first entered this ministry, I approached an elderly saint in the church about a difficulty I experienced after praying. I said, "Sister Ramsey, I spend two hours praying for special needs but as soon as I enter the day, discouragement comes from every direction. What is wrong?" Her response has long since ministered to me. "When you get off your knees, take Jesus with you. Don't leave him behind." Surely in his presence is fullness of joy. We must take him with us.

A few months ago, I found myself frustrated over an event I couldn't change. It stole my joy. I continually complained to God over my demise. Finally, he answered, *Lisa, there is a golden nugget here if you'll search for it.* I mumbled further about nothing good possibly coming from this situation, but eventually withdrew when I realized my complaining accomplished little. I should at least try trusting. For over a week I petitioned God concerning the golden nugget. One Sunday morning before service while at the height of my anxiety a thought entered. *The first commandment says to love the Lord your God with all of your heart, your mind, your soul, and your strength. What does the second one say?* I responded by saying. "It is to love my neighbor as myself." *This is the golden nugget.*

Much to my amazement, that morning my husband opened his text by reading, "Love your neighbor as yourself." The anxiety left and joy returned as I began to love the person who brought me such frustration.

While 1 Corinthians 13 helps us define love, Romans 8:37–39 presents us with a visual image of God's love that flows through us.

> No, in all these things we are more than conquerors through him who loved us. For I am convinced that neither death nor life, neither angels nor demons, neither the present nor the future, nor any powers, neither height nor depth, nor anything else in all creation, will be able to separate us from the love of God that is in Christ Jesus our Lord.

Surely if we have God's love inside of us, what can separate us from one another? Love is an unbreakable bond. When this bond of love is established, watch out, Satan. He fights us most to prevent us from establishing relationships rooted in the love of God.

When we love, we receive joy to overcome. When we love, we're more forgiving. When we love, we're more apt to overlook faults in others. When we love, we learn to lighten up and take ourselves a little less serious. When we love, we learn to laugh a little more. When we love, we walk the land with the eyes of Christ.

Strength to Finish the Task

When I was first married, a late freeze killed our bushes. Something needed to be done to replace them. My husband jokingly said, "If you remove those bushes, you can have whatever you want in the front yard." Unbeknownst to him, he had presented a challenge I couldn't resist. The following week I set out with a mattock and a shovel to uproot the dead bushes.

I preached the finest sermons ever heard to the bees, bugs, flies, spiders, and ants as I dug away. The joy of the Lord so consumed me I hardly noticed the enormity of the task. *One bush. I'm going to plant whatever I want. Two bushes. Give me strength, Lord Jesus. Three bushes. My husband will be impressed. One to go. With the Lord by my side I can make it the extra mile. Our front yard will be beautiful. Praise the Lord.*

When my husband arrived from work that evening he saw the bushes beside the curb. He came into the house laughing. "Who did you get to remove the bushes?" Proudly, I raised my hand. Throughout the evening he insisted that I tell him who helped me. He couldn't believe I cut through the large roots. I repeatedly refuted him. Finally, he conceded and said, "Well, it looks like I have a real corn woman on my hands."

"Yes, and one who receives a lot of help from Jesus," was my response.

Truly the joy of the Lord is our strength. It's like gasoline in our tank, or bleach in our wash, or a shot of caffeine, or high-wattage light bulbs, or an extra pair of hands. A job we think is impossible is infused with creativity and energy when we have his presence behind us. Our conversations become renewed with an influx of possibilities.

Fear Steals Joy

During the months leading up to Steve's death, I took long walks. As I walked, I held long conversations with God. One day vividly stands out.

I said, "Okay, Lord, which way today?" I waited for his response.

How about the lake route today? I have something to show you.

As I walked along the lake path I saw a dead bird. I said, "Oh Lord, I hate death."

I know.

"Why do we have to die?"

So you can live.

"I hate death."

I know.

But this particular conversation didn't end this day. It resumed again several months later. Steve was in the hospital intensive care unit. I was given special permission from his doctor to sleep in a lounging chair next to his bed. Every morning at 6 o'clock the nurse came to conduct tests and I went to the chapel to pray. On this morning, in great turmoil, I cried out to God, "Why don't you heal him?"

Life is in the spirit.

I didn't want to hear what he was saying. Loudly, I continued to petition him. "Life is in the spirit but it is also in the physical body. Why don't you heal him?"

Life is in the spirit.

I stood, grabbed my purse with a tape player inside, and left the hospital to take a walk. Angrily I placed the headphones to my ears and listened to the soothing music while I attempted to calm my anxious spirit. After two laps around the outside of the hospital I began to cry.

Lisa, why are you afraid?

"God, I'm afraid of losing him. I don't want to lose him. What will I do without him? I can't do this."

Trust me.

And I did—eventually.

Why was I afraid? Uncertainty? Regardless of the root of my fear, it would steal my joy and render me ineffective because fear opposes faith. I needed to surrender my fear by confessing, inspecting, and repenting of it.

I confessed my fear much the way I did when asked what I was afraid of. I recognized the existence of fear before I even hoped to be free of it. At the hospital when God confronted me with his question, my confession released peace.

Occasionally, I have to pull weeds around our flowers and shrubbery. The weeds begin to die when the roots are pulled out of the ground and exposed to air. As I confessed my fears, I exposed the root that released me from imprisonment. While the journey to recovery was not complete with the confession, it was the starting place.

Once I confessed my fear, I analyzed it. Through examination, I discovered even though my fears require serious consideration, fear isn't the solution. Scripture admonishes me that a double-minded man is unstable in everything. Trusting God is the answer.

Has this conversation brought to mind a fear that may be stealing your joy and blocking your faith in God? Confess it now. Lay your hand over your heart and the other one to heaven.

> Lord, I confess my fear to you. I admit that I have been afraid of _____.
> I've been unable to move beyond it. This fear has destroyed my relationship with you and with others. Now as I confess my fear I receive your grace that is sufficient for the days ahead. I can make it with your help. I choose to trust you.

Allow his joy to fill your heart. Make peace with God. Trust him.

Silence

A teenage boy who lived in our neighborhood played his music so loud it vibrated the windows of our house. I wondered about his parents and the neighbors on either side of them. I even wondered about the health of his eardrums. It seems that we can't get away from noise, even to relax.

My friend Angie was raising four boys under the age of eight. "My house is noisy all the time," she told me. "Sometimes I go into the bathroom and hide just to experience a moment of peace. But without fail, my two-year-old will find me and sit at the door and wail until I exit."

Karen Linamen offers an interesting observation along these lines.

> It's nice to be sought after. But sometimes you can get too much of a good thing. My pet peeve is hearing a knock on the bathroom door followed by the familiar words, "What are you doing in there?"
>
> What do they think I'm doing?
>
> Maybe kids have this weird fear that, while their bathroom time is reserved for boring functions of elimination, grown-ups aren't bound by the same rules. Maybe they think we hide out in the bathroom so we can do really cool things we don't let them do, like eating Gummi Bears before dinner and watching cartoons when our homework isn't done. That's why we lock the door. We don't want our children to know we're having all the fun.[3]

☙☙

Robert's wife, Schaunell, died of cancer the year after my husband, Steve, died. It was several years later that Robert and I met and were married. Robert has two children, Torrey and Latese. They were raised in an environment that appreciates silence. Our first Christmas together was unbelievably quiet. All evening, Joe and I exchanged panicked expressions. We thought we'd go out of our minds. Once we entered another room where we couldn't be heard, we both released horrified exclamations. "This is the quietest Christmas I've ever experienced!"

As life would have it, both Torrey and Latese married into families who were both loud. Their spouses, Polly and Philip (along with me), have added a little life to this black-tie affair—even if they think we are ill-mannered for doing so. Eventually, Torrey and Latese had children and life changed dramatically. The children supply all the fun. Yes, it's the grandchildren who refuse to allow us to hide in the bathroom. "What are you doing in there?"

An interesting thing happened when the loud and the quiet began to mix. We learned to appreciate both in their unique ways. Sometimes, I think my husband actually likes the noise. I know I enjoy the silence. But Latese abandoned ship and went completely the other way. She thrives in the commotion. She's like a bird released from a cage. It's fun to watch. But please let me have a few minutes of peace and quiet. We'll stay up all night tomorrow.

Torrey is another matter. He's neither loud nor overly demonstrative. He just laughs—at us.

Regardless of our station in life, we need quiet. Silence is the birthing place of joy. It's in the silence we commune with God. But silence is too confrontational for some. It brings us face to face with things we don't want to admit about ourselves. We'd rather live in the safety of noise. We hope noise will drown out our sorrow and perhaps our sin and give us cause to feel good.

The loud music, jumping, running, dancing, and clapping do not necessarily indicate the presence of joy. I knew a man who did all these things in church while he repeatedly committed adultery. While I appreciate lively music and like to clap and dance with joy, I most experience God's presence when my soul is still before him.

"Be still and know that I am God" (Psalm 46:10).

I Can Do Something About This

I can do everything through him who gives me strength
(Philippians 4:3)

Pray
Dearest Lord,
I need joy. Joy causes me to overlook the faults in others,
to become less irritated with the insignificant issues, and to
have a sense of liberty. I desire to spend more time in quiet so that
this joy is birthed. For in your presence is fullness of joy. I make
room in my heart for you so that my joy may be complete.

Consider
Think of seven people who might benefit from a word of
encouragement. Write these names on a sheet of paper.
(This person may be a neighbor, coworker,
former teacher, boss, or family member.)

Think
Next to the names of these people, write something
positive about them, such as faithfulness, generosity,
compassion, joyfulness, energy, godliness, honesty,
or willingness to help when needed.

Write
Every day, write one of these people and express your
feelings about them. Tell her how much she has meant
to you. If appropriate, pick a wildflower and present
it to her as an expression of your appreciation. You
may want to involve your child in this presentation.
She could paint a rock or make a card.

Meditate

How did this note make me feel? Did it bring joy?
What will my greater love reveal?
Pockets full of gold secretly concealed?
Power or possessions within my reach?
My garden—every orchid, every peach?
Is it solely those who love that lose?
My heart cries it must be much of what I choose.

Some favor a rosy path, some forgotten avenues.
Some desire much silver, some just a few.
Some seek freedom, some to possess the land.
Some labor tirelessly, some simply stand.
Some follow their dream, some to get by.
Some fight to live, some hope to die.

In agony I grasp for the truth of greater gain,
And travail my ambitions, please not to live in vain.
The dawning approaches lighting latter years
The unveiling to unmask sweat, blood, tears.
Was my life to live for me?
Was my life spent all for Thee?

—LISA Q. HERRIN ©1984

Conclusion

I'VE BEEN LOVED by somebody all of my life. How would I have known to love if somebody hadn't first loved me, held me, protected me, nourished me? This love has transformed me, empowered me, sustained me, and released me through many dark days.

For me, love began at home. I've talked about my mother, but you've yet to meet Dad. He taught me to sew, crochet, knit and pearl, wallpaper, type, and garden. Every spring, we connected in the garden.

I enjoyed dropping the corn seeds. He dug the holes and fertilized while I followed with the seed. I couldn't understand how one seed made such a huge stalk, so occasionally I deposited a handful. This repeated itself for a number of years.

Twenty-five years later, I felt a need to confess my dirty deed to Dad. He looked at me, popped me on the arm, and said, "I know you did, you little rascal. Every year I said, 'That Lisa, look what she's done.'" If I know my dad, I believed he had a good laugh every year in the cornfield.

But one day I left my parents and became joined to a love of a different kind—that of marriage. Steve filled my world with flowers of every description, whether picked by the roadside, around a fishing pond, or from a 7-Eleven. He gave me much to laugh about and contemplate.

During the last weeks of his life he said, "When I get well I'm not going to buy flowers for you anymore. I'm going to plant them all around this house so everywhere you look you will be surrounded by my love for you." He never got a chance to plant the flowers.

When he died I wondered who would bring me flowers, surprise me with PayDay candy bars, and sing crazy off-key songs. And who would pay a photographer to follow me around Bermuda for a picture to frame. And who would wrap my presents in cartoon paper with the date placed so he'd know if I attempted a peek. And who would think to buy a huge fishing tackle box to perfectly place my sewing notions. And who would buy our son the first car when the bike days were over, the Boy Scout knife was too juvenile, and the BB gun too small? What would happen when his love was gone?

After Steve died, Joe and I planted flowers around the house. I gathered favorite pictures and enlarged and framed them. I carefully dusted around his computer, briefcase, and resoled shoes. And daily, I peeked into his closet to see if his favorite shirts and jacket were still in place. At Christmas I purchased my own gifts, wrapped them, and placed them under the tree from him. But these were all fillers for an empty crater. This wouldn't always suffice.

The time came when yesterday didn't work anymore. I gathered the remaining remnants of our life together in a box: the shoes, razor, brush, briefcase, playing cards, shirts, and jacket. With the closing of the box, the funeral began again. How many times did I need to bury him? Wasn't once enough? I placed it in the attic for Joe.

I'd lost my best friend forever. Two years after his death, the agony continued as the turmoil over what I'd lost shrouded anything good that might enter. My nightly ritual consisted of my complaints to God: "I've lost my lover. Joe's lost his dad. We've lost our family, our happiness, our future." But then one day like Job, God had heard enough and He responded. *These are not what you have lost, but what you've gained.*

Love

I am strengthened by the words former President Ronald Reagan delivered at a eulogy in a hangar in Kentucky on December 1985 to the family members of an Army transport plane carrying 248 soldiers that had crashed during takeoff in Gander, Newfoundland. Everyone died.

> You were a part of them. And just as you think today of the joy they gave you, think for a moment of the joy you gave them, and be glad. For love is never wasted, love is never lost; love lives on and sees us through sorrow. From the moment love is born it is always with us, keeping us aloft in the flooding and strong in the time of trial.[1]

An invaluable experience presents itself to us in the world of love. If we've been loved and if we've been given the opportunity to love, we are most rich. We've not lost but greatly gained. Love is an experience that can never be stripped from us. It not only stays with us, but also is duplicated as we in turn give this gift to others.

When I learned to see my marriage as an experience of love that I gained, I saw my aging parents, siblings, and son and thanked God for every opportunity to share a memory of love. This gratitude emerged without fear that one day they might be taken from me as well. Oftentimes, we forget this life is temporary. I look at a picture on the counter of my mother and Joe and say, "Thank you, Lord, that she came to see me Mother's Day. What a wonderful experience. This may never happen again. But the special nature of this memory can never be taken from me."

As imperfect people, we might not be able to say we've been loved perfectly. Who but God can love without flaw? While others do not love us perfectly, we don't always love others as well as we should. We all experience moments of selfishness and even our generosity eventually reveals impure motives.

Perhaps you've never felt love emanate, not from even a single individual. Somehow you've fallen through cracks in the floor. You feel you've been dropped and left to die alone. Please don't be fooled forever. You are loved. Jesus loves you. He's launched a massive army all around waiting to love you. But first you have to say yes. You must give him permission to enter your front door. Then you must allow his people to love you. You'll find that when you do, someday you'll stop saying you've never been loved. For not only will you feel love, you will be compelled to give love. This is what happens when you experience love. You return it. You begin something that will continue to bless others.

Children

For better or for worse our children reflect us. How can we not love them? When Joe was small, he had a favorite friend, a stuffed clown named Boling. Boling went with Joe on trips in the car and to the park, mall, or grocery store. Boling was a good listener, a confidant, and took all sorts of abuse. I wanted to secret him away and replace him with a new one, to which his dad adamantly objected. "It won't be the same," he said.

Joe's bed was full at night with his Bible, Boling, and whatever new item he felt he needed to create a haven for sleep. When his dad died, Joe's affinity with Boling grew stronger. Boling filled new places a young boy couldn't adequately explain. But I knew it wasn't enough. Stuffed clowns, pets, and dolls can't replace a breathing soul.

Boling took Steve's place on the swing, water slide, and ball field. Boling and Joe had a game all their own into which not even I fit.

Two months after Steve's death, Joe began crying loudly, almost in hysterics, as we left his grandparents' house for our four-hour drive back home. I'd never seen Joe act this way. He repeatedly screamed, "I want my grandma!" as he pounded his hands against the dashboard and stomped his feet on the floor of the car. I didn't know how to handle his bizarre behavior. I silently prayed as I continued to drive.

"Lord, what do I do?"

When I found a safe place to stop, I pulled the car over to the side of the road and waited for him to calm down. Through his tears I heard something I hadn't heard before; although he repeatedly screamed "I want my grandma!" In my heart I heard the words he couldn't give himself permission to verbalize—"I want my daddy." His dad had been taken from him and he felt powerless. I knew I needed to infuse him with a new sense of control.

When he had calmed down, I said, "Joe, I think you are telling me you feel powerless. You feel you don't have any choices. I'm giving you a choice now. You said you looked forward to returning to school in Virginia Beach because you want to play basketball this year. But if this is not what you want, I will sell our house and move back home to live near Grandma. This is your choice."

He sat with his head down, clutching Boling to his side and said, "I want to go back to Virginia Beach to play basketball." We hugged each other and cried.

Upon releasing him, I looked into his little face and said, "I miss Daddy too."

But the healing didn't end here. We had other obstacles to overcome. He came running into my bedroom one morning and said, "Mama, I dreamed Daddy died and that you were going to die too." Years later, he confessed that he had cried in bed many nights for fear I would die.

"Yes, Joe your daddy died. But you know what? Even though it hurts, God helps us. I can't promise you I will live forever, but I can say that no matter what happens, God will always help us. You will never be destitute."

We have a purpose to fulfill. I embrace God's purpose for my life. As I've said before, neither my son nor I will leave until this purpose has been served. Without fear I can love the people God has brought into my life knowing he will keep them there until his purpose is fulfilled. I am free to enjoy life with those I love.

A New Day—A New Love

I look back to when all seemed up for question. I did not feel God would ever bring anyone else to love me. Fear kept me enslaved in doubt. I wondered if God had rejected me. On March 10, 1992, my journal entry read:

> God, I am so lonely. Will you wrap your arms around me? I need to feel warmth. My soul cries out for comfort and I'm screaming for relief. I cannot have my way no matter how loud or long I cry. Temper tantrums change nothing. You are not impressed with my emotional outrage. You know my every angle to persuade. My energy is wasted on You.
>
> I must give up my ridiculous hopes and be content with singleness. I must allow you to re-establish my course.
>
> Oh God, I want someone special to love. I cannot stop wanting it. I want back what was stolen from me. Love. Romance. Please help me to stop wanting these things if I'm never allowed to have them again. You'll have to do this because I don't know how to stop wanting it. Although I'm having difficulty living these two years as a single parent, I know your grace is altogether sufficient and I trust You to do what is best.
>
> Please give me hope for the future. Please root out the enormity of this despair so that I may survive. Please teach me to wait.

On my kitchen counter stands a beautiful floral arrangement from a special man I've been married to now for over twelve years. They are an arrangement of a different sort—unusual in kind and color. I look at them and my heart over-flows with gratitude that I possess this opportunity to love one more time. The flowers were a gift from Robert congratulating me on my writing achievements. He reflects God's love to me in the simplest of ways—a sentimental card, an afternoon walk, a shared laugh, a love song—his song to me.

Robert's wife also died from cancer. We share a common experience—suffering. He is the reason I'm writing this book. He so strongly believed in my writing he encouraged me to return to college, participate in a writing program, and attend writers conferences.

We talk about heaven a lot and wonder what our former spouses are doing. Robert says I have a more vivid imagination, because I firmly believe Steve is happily building houses for the arrival of his family. Robert thinks Schaunell is serving—I think she's serving glasses of lemonade to the builders.

Our children are free to talk about their parents and grandparents. Noah is ten years old and he is the son of Robert's son, Torrey. When Noah was five, I asked him to share the tradition of decorating the Christmas tree as I shared with Joe before he went away to college.

We pulled all the ornaments from the boxes and carefully laid them on the floor. As we hung the ornaments, we took turns deciding which ornament represented each family member. We first hung an ornament in celebration of Jesus' birthday. He decided upon an angel to represent Schaunell. He explained that he was placing her high upon the tree because she's in heaven. I asked him to choose an ornament to hang in memory of Joe's father, Steve. He chose another sort of angel and hung him down toward the bottom of the tree. I asked him why he placed him so low. He said, "Because he is dead." I guess that doesn't mean he thinks Steve is also in heaven. Our family had a good laugh over his logic.

God gave us the opportunity to love and be loved again. We are not in competition with a former spouse nor do we want our children to feel the memory of their parent is being threatened. We have good relationships with our former in-laws. Robert's former mother-in-law once introduced me as her daughter-in-law and it seemed fitting, because she's always made me feel like one.

The best benefit of all is that I've inherited three beautiful grandchildren and I love each one of them as if they were my own flesh and blood. Since Joe never had brothers and sisters, he especially enjoys being an uncle. The little girls have him wrapped twice around their finger—even when they take possession of his chair to watch television, keep him up late at night, or when Noah wants him to play catch for two hours.

God has been so good to us.

Notes

Chapter 1

1. Dag Hammarskjöld, *Markings* (New York: Alfred A. Knopf, 1964), 100, 118.

2. Joanna Weaver, *Having a Mary Heart in a Martha World* (Colorado Springs, CO: Waterbrook Press, 2000), 91. Used with permission.

3. Jerry Cook and Stanley C. Baldwin, *Love, Acceptance, and Forgiveness* (Ventura, CA: Regal Books, 1979), 97. Used with permission.

4. Nancy Leigh DeMoss, *Lies Women Believe* (Chicago: Moody Press, 2001), 118-119. Used with permission.

Chapter 2

1. Karen Scalf Linamen, *Just Hand Over the Chocolate and No One Will Get Hurt* (Grand Rapids, MI: Revell, 1999), 95.

2. Mike Huckabee, *Character Is the Issue* (Nashville, TN: Broadman & Holman, 1997), 88. Used with permission.

3. Drs. Henry Cloud & John Townsend, *God Will Make a Way* (Nashville, TN: Integrity Publishers, 1997), 170. Used with permission.

Chapter 3

1. Henry Wadsworth Longfellow, *The Poetical Works of Longfellow* (Boston: Houghton Mifflin Company, 1975), 290.

2. John Foxe, *The New Foxe's Book of Martyrs* (Gainesville, FL: Bridge-Logos, 2001), 6-8.

3. David Barrett, ed., *World Christian Encyclopedia* (New York: Oxford University Press, 1981).

Chapter 4

1. Rudyard Kipling, *Rudyard Kipling's Verse* (Garden City, NY: Doubleday and Company, 1940), 226.

2. Charles Swindoll, *Growing Old in the Seasons of Life* (Portland, OR: Multnomah Publishers, 1983), 51, 53.

3. Drs. Henry Cloud & John Townsend, *God Will Make a Way* (Nashville, TN: Integrity Publishers, 2002), 74. Used with permission.

4. Ruth Senter, *Have We Really Come a Long Way?* (Minneapolis: Bethany House, 1997), 134, 135.

5. Robert E. Fisher, *The Joy of Relationship* (Cleveland, TN: Pathway Press, 1997), 37. Used with permission.

Chapter 5

1. Henry Longfellow, *Henry Wadsworth Longfellow, Evangeline* (New York: Penguin Group, 1964), 185.

2. Calvin Miller, *Once Upon a Tree* (West Monroe, LA: Howard Publishing, 2002),132, 133. Used with permission.

3. Mark Buchanan, *Things Unseen* (Sisters, OR: Multnomah Publishers, 2002), 204. Used with permission.

4. Ibid., 9. Used with permission.

5. Peggy Noonan, *On Speaking Well* (New York: HarperCollins Publishers, 1998), 172. Used with permission.

6. Peter Marshall, *John Doe, Disciple* (New York: McGraw Hill, 1963), 219, 220.

7. John Maxwell and Jim Dornan, *Becoming a Person of Influence* (Nashville, TN: Thomas Nelson Publishers, 1997), 55, 56.

8. Charles W. Conn, *When Your Upright World Turns Upside Down* (Cleveland, TN: Pathway Press, 1990), 57. Used with permission.

Chapter 7

1. Louisa May Alcott, *The Poems of Louisa May Alcott* (New York: Ironweed Press, 2000), 131.

2. Drs. Henry Cloud & John Townsend, *God Will Make a Way* (Nashville, TN: Integrity Publishers, 2002), 78. Used with permission.

3. Philip Yancey, *Soul Survivor* (New York: Doubleday, 2001), 77, 78.

4. Carol Terry Talbott and Virginia Muir, *Escape at Dawn* (Wheaton, IL: Tyndale House Publishers, 1988).

5. Calvin Miller, *Once Upon a Tree* (West Monroe, LA: Howard Publishing, 2002), 8. Used with permission.

Chapter 8

1. John Bartlett, *Bartlett's Familiar Quotations* (New York: Little, Brown and Company, 1992), 309.

Chapter 9

1. Jim Ryun et al, *Heroes among Us* (Shippensburg, PA: Destiny Image, 2002), 15, 16.

2. Ravi Zacharias, *Light in the Shadow of Jihad* (Sisters, OR: Multnomah Publishers, 2002), 92.

Chapter 11

1. Emily Dickinson, *Favorite Poems of Emily Dickinson* (New York: Avenal Books, 1890), 41.

2. Martha Bolton, *I Think Therefore I Have a Headache* (Minneapolis: Bethany House, 2003), 182, 183.

3. Karen Scalf Linamen, *Just Hand Over the Chocolate and No One Will Get Hurt* (Grand Rapids, MI: Revell, 1999), 94.

Chapter 12

1. Peggy Noonan, *On Speaking Well* (New York: HarperCollins, 1998), 173. Used with permission.